BACK TO THE BASICS:
WINNING IS MORE THAN X'S AND O'S

Coach John L. Meadows

Coach John L. Meadows

with

Coach Doug Styles

Extra Point Publishing
Hazel Green, Alabama

BACK TO THE BASICS: WINNING IS MORE THAN X'S AND O'S

Copyright © 2008 by John L. Meadows

All rights reserved.
No part of this publication may be reproduced or transmitted in any form or by any means, electronic or mechanical, without the written permission of the publisher.

Published by Extra Point Publishing

All brand names used herein are registered trademarks of their respective owners. Reference herein to any specific commercial product, process, or service by trade name, trademark, manufacturer, or otherwise, does not necessarily constitute or imply its endorsement, recommendation, or favoring by the authors or Extra Point Publishing.

ISBN-13: 978-0-9820457-0-1
ISBN-10: 0-9820457-0-0

PRINTED IN THE UNITED STATES OF AMERICA

1 2 3 4 5 6 7 8 9 10

To Glenda

Contents

INTRODUCTION xix

FOREWORD xxiii

ABOUT THE AUTHOR xxv

PREFACE xxix

ACKNOWLEDGMENTS xxxi

Part I
Essential Elements in Developing a Championship Program

Chapter 1—Creating an Atmosphere in a Community That Expects To Win Because Of You and Your Program 3

    Selling Your Program 3

    Providing the Best Instruction Possible on the Football Field 5

    Familiarizing Your Coaches with Every Phase of the Game and Encouraging Them in Developing an Inquisitive Mind and a Total Dedication to the Game 5

    Developing and Displaying a Positive, Outgoing Attitude Necessary in Recognizing the Potential That Lies Within Those We Coach ... 6

    Assigning Coaching Duties According To Their Knowledge, Abilities, and Experience 6

    Involving Active and Positive Members of the Community in Your Program 7

    Soliciting and Earning the Confidence and Support of Administration, Staff, and Students 8

Developing the Team Through Off-Season Duties and Responsibilities 9

PART II
THE COACH AS A COUNSELOR

Chapter 2—Coaching Responsibilities That Do Not Involve Football 13

    Defining the Coach 13

    Addressing Individual Problems of the Teenager 13

        Family Problems 14

        Social Problems—Football: The Great Equalizer 15

        Financial Problems 16

        Psychological Problems 18

        School Problems 20

PART III
CHARACTER TRAITS OF THE COACH WHO IS A TRUE LEADER

Chapter 3—Qualities for the Coach To Develop for Success 25

    Integrity 25

    Friendship 25

    Courage 25

    Exemplary Work Ethic 26

    Perseverance 26

    Loyalty 26

    Thoroughness 26

    Humility 27

    Wisdom 27

PART IV
DIVINE WISDOM

Chapter 4—Divine Wisdom: Defined by James 3:16–17 and Applied to the Coaching Profession 31

    Biblical Principles of Wisdom 31

        Pure 31

        Peaceable 31

        Gentle 31

        Reasonable 31

        Full of Mercy 31

        Full of Good Fruits 32

        Unwavering 32

        Without Hypocrisy 32

        Conclusion 32

PART V
ATTITUDES TO BE DEVELOPED IN THE WINNING ATHLETE

Chapter 5—Intrinsic Values To Instill and To Expand in Our Athletes 35

    Academics 35

    Dedication 35

    Team-Player Attitude 35

    Drive and Determination 36

    Leadership (Servant) 37

    Competitiveness 38

    Confidence 38

    Discipline 39

Realism 39

Toughness—Physical and Mental 40

PART VI
TIPS FOR VICTORY

Chapter 6—Guidelines I've Used Through the Years 45

Match Up Players 45

As Much As Possible, Have Somebody on the Center 48

Scout Yourself 49

Teach Your Linemen Every Offensive-Line Position 49

Align Your Best Blockers According To Defensive Set 50

Set Your Offense To Set Their Defense 50

Have an In-Depth Scouting Report Against Best Opponents 50

Don't Be So Proud That You Can't—or Won't—Learn from Other Coaches 51

Don't Outsmart Yourself 51

PART VII
DEVELOPING A SIMPLE, EFFECTIVE, AND FLEXIBLE GAME PLAN

Chapter 7—Scouting Your Opponent 55

Personal Observation 55

Films/Tapes 56

Newspaper Articles/Visits 57

Phone Calls 57

Part VIII
Defensive Fundamentals of the Game

Chapter 8—Defensive Philosophy 61
- Stunting 61
- Triangular Read 63
- Stopping Certain Popular Plays with a 5–3 Triangular Read 66
- Special Defenses 73
- 5–3 Variations 76

Chapter 9—Selection of Personnel 79
- Defensive Linemen 79
- Defensive Ends 80
- Linebackers 81
- Defensive Backs (With Drills Used for Selection) 83
- Pass-Defense Drills 87

Part IX
Offensive Fundamentals of the Game

Chapter 10—Offensive Philosophy 95
- Diversity 95
- Offensive-Line Blocking Schemes 96
- Power Blocking 106
- Blocking by Backs on Ends and Linebackers 109
- Blocking by Wide Receivers 115
- Most Successful Plays 117
- Passing Package 125

Screen-Pass Blocking Rules 128
Play-Action Pass Protection 130
Sprint-Out Pass Protection 132
Three-Step Drop Pass Protection 136

Chapter 11—Offensive Personnel 161
Selection of Personnel 161
    Quarterbacks 161
    Offensive Line 162
    Tight Ends 164
    Receivers 164
    Running Backs 165

PART X
AFTER THE FINAL WHISTLE

Chapter 12—Off-Season Program 169
Evaluation 169
Individual Meetings 172
Goal Setting 173
Strength Training 174
Skill Training 175
Spring Training 176
Summertime 178
    Grades 178
    Girls 178
    Cars 179
    Allied Van Lines 179
    Better Offer 180

Chapter 13—Getting It All Together 183
Practice Schedule 183
Pre-Game Walk-Through 184

PART XI
THE REASON THAT IT ALL CAME TO PASS

The Number One Key to My Success 189

FIGURES

Figure	8–1	5–3 Tackles Pinch	61
Figure	8–2	Off-Tackle Play	62
Figure	8–3	Triangular Read	64
Figure	8–4	5–3 Triangular-Read	65
Figure	8–5	Even Trap	67
Figure	8–6	Lead	68
Figure	8–7	Zone	69
Figure	8–8	Power	70
Figure	8–9	Sweep	71
Figure	8–10	Inside Veer	72
Figure	8–11	Dallas Strong	73
Figure	8–12	Dallas Strong, Tackles Flare	74
Figure	8–13	Bird's Eye 50	74
Figure	8–14	Bird's Eye 60	75
Figure	8–15	Bird's Eye 44	75
Figure	8–16	Flat Slant	76
Figure	8–17	Cut Slant	76
Figure	8–18	Penetrating Slant	77
Figure	8–19	Eight-Man Blitz	77
Figure	8–20	Middle Blitz—Tackles Cut Ends	77
Figure	8–21	Tackles Pinch	78
Figure	9–1	Special Defense—Stud Linebacker	83
Figure	9–2	Pass Defender Drill	88
Figure	9–3	Man-to-Man Drill	89
Figure	9–4	Man-and-One Drill	90
Figure	9–5	React and Score Drill	91
Figure	10–1	Overblock	97
Figure	10–2	Stance	98
Figure	10–3	No Vertical Splits	99
Figure	10–4	Good Vertical Splits	99
Figure	10–5	Zone Drill	102
Figure	10–6	Zone Read Right	102
Figure	10–7	Guard Around Center	103
Figure	10–8	Tackle Around Guard	103
Figure	10–9	Double A-Gap Man	104
Figure	10–10	Double B-Gap Man	104
Figure	10–11	Double C-Gap Man	105
Figure	10–12	End Around Tackle	105
Figure	10–13	Double-Team Blocking	106
Figure	10–14	Backer-Backer-Safety	106
Figure	10–15	Blocked by Alignment	107

Figure 10-16	Tight End's Rule	107
Figure 10-17	X Block	108
Figure 10-18	Regular Block	109
Figure 10-19	Even Front Drill	111
Figure 10-20	Odd Front Drill	112
Figure 10-21	Tackle Pinches	112
Figure 10-22	Tackle Slants Out	113
Figure 10-23	Defensive End Blocking	113
Figure 10-24	Kick-Out or Seal	114
Figure 10-25	Hitting the Bubble	114
Figure 10-26	End-Pinch Read	115
Figure 10-27	Stack I—Power Off-Tackle	117
Figure 10-28	Stack I Double Lead	120
Figure 10-29	Stack I Fullback Wedge	122
Figure 10-30	Double-Screen Read	124
Figure 10-31	Counter Bootleg	126
Figure 10-32	Standing Overblock	126
Figure 10-33	Read Backside Rush	127
Figure 10-34	Fake Counter Bootleg Screen to TB	128
Figure 10-35	Counter Bootleg Read	129
Figure 10-36	Versus 4-4	131
Figure 10-37	"Hot Route"	131
Figure 10-38	Sprint Right	132
Figure 10-39	Defensive End Squeezes Hole or Boxes	133
Figure 10-40	X Lead Against Boxing End	133
Figure 10-41	Scramble-Out Route	134
Figure 10-42	Sprint-Right Wheel Route	135
Figure 10-43	Sprint-Right Wheel Comeback	135
Figure 10-44	Sprint-Right Slant Out/Read	136
Figure 10-45	Three-Step Protection	137
Figure 10-46	Three-Step Protection for 50	137
Figure 10-47	Pass 1	138
Figure 10-48	Pass 2	139
Figure 10-49	Cover 3	140
Figure 10-50	Cover 2	141
Figure 10-51	Pass 4	142
Figure 10-52	Pass 5 – Cover 3	143
Figure 10-53	Cover 2	143
Figure 10-54	Pass 6	144
Figure 10-55	Pass 7	144
Figure 10-56	Stack I Counter Trap	145
Figure 10-57	Swap Block	145
Figure 10-58	Backer-Backer Safety for Trap	146
Figure 10-59	Blocking X Stunt – Center Covered	146

Figure 10–60 Trapping Stunting Linebacker 147
Figure 10–61 Quarterback Suicide 148
Figure 10–62 Reverse 149
Figure 10–63 Reverse – Unbalanced Line 150
Figure 10–64 Reverse – Wing Set 150
Figure 10–65 Unbalanced Line Toss Sweep 151
Figure 10–66 Fake Toss Sweep 152
Figure 10–67 Sprint Right—Screen to Left End 153
Figure 10–68 Fake Power Left—Bootleg Pick 154
Figure 10–69 Pick Play with Motion 157
Figure 10–70 Pick on Backside Backer 157
Figure 10–71 Fake Field Goal 158
Figure 10–72 End-Around Reverse Kickoff Return 159

ABBREVIATIONS

B – Back
C – Center or Corner Back
DB – Defensive Back
DT – Defensive Tackle
E – End
FB – Fullback
FS – Free Safety
G – Guard
K – Kicker
LB – Linebacker
LG – Left Guard
LH – Left Hash Line
LOS – Line of Scrimmage
LT – Left Tackle
M – "Mike" – Middle Linebacker
MD – Mid-field Hash Line
N, NG – Nose Guard
NB – Nickel Back
PP – Personal Protector
Q, QB – Quarterback
RG – Right Guard
RH – Right Hash Line
RT – Right Tackle
S – "Sam" – Strong-side Linebacker
SS – Strong Safety
T – Tackle
TB – Tailback
TE – Tight end
W – "Will" – Weak-side Linebacker
WB – Wing Back
X – Split End
Y – Tight End
Z – Flanker

INTRODUCTION

I was flattered and pleased when legendary high school football coach John Meadows asked me to write an introduction to *BACK TO THE BASICS: Winning Is More Than X's and O's*. But I was even more pleased to learn a few months ago that this book was being written in the first place. Many of us who followed John Meadows' storied career over the years often mentioned to him and to others that he should commit at least some of his vast football knowledge to the printed page. And now, in collaboration with his longtime friend and associate Doug Styles, that's exactly what he has done.

The coaches who delve into the technical portions of this book will come away with a far greater understanding of the game and how to teach it than they ever knew before. That's a guarantee. Equally as important, they'll discover that winning in football, as in life, truly is much more than X's and O's.

Both my parents were schoolteachers, and if the profession I had chosen fresh out of college had been teaching and coaching instead of journalism, I couldn't have hoped to learn from a better instructor than John Meadows. Nor could a rookie sportswriter in the mid-1960s have wished for a better subject to observe, to study, to admire, and to write about than John Meadows.

I first met the man in 1965 when he came to Huntsville's Butler High School after winning a state championship at Scottsboro. A native of Falkville in Morgan County and a graduate of Jacksonville State University, Meadows had already been a highly successful head coach at Hanceville and Gordo before moving on to Scottsboro and eventually to Butler where he quickly turned a sagging program into one of the best in the state. Years later, after leaving Butler, he did the same thing just across the state line at Lincoln County High School in Tennessee where he became one of only a handful of coaches ever to win a state championship in two neighboring states.

The title of this book, *BACK TO THE BASICS*, was aptly chosen. Right from the start, John Meadows believed that winning football teams always won because they were carefully and systematically schooled in the basics of blocking and tackling. "We ran a few drills in practice," one of his former players once told me, "but mostly we just scrimmaged. Coach Meadows wanted to find out who could block and tackle." Meadows' teams were never fancy. Defensively, they swarmed and gang-tackled. Offensively, they blocked and ran the football, usually between the tackles in keeping with the head coach's popular nickname, "Off-Tackle John." Occasionally, they'd throw a pass or two. Mostly, they won. The pages of this book offer a textbook clinic on how they did it. Personally, what I'll remember most about John Meadows is not how they did it but the way he went about it. Most of his contemporaries ran carefully structured practices, going from one timed period to another. Meadows' teams didn't require much structure. Mostly, they just went out and scrimmaged because the head coach wanted to find out who could block and tackle.

I remember one mid-week autumn afternoon in the '60s. Butler was getting ready to play Huntsville High, its biggest rival. Huntsville's coach was another of the state's best and most intense coaches, Tom Owen. The day before, I'd visited Huntsville's practice, which was meticulously organized down to the last detail. The Crimson Panthers looked and acted like a college team. Tom Owen left nothing to chance. When I showed up ten minutes into Butler's practice the next afternoon, the team was already scrimmaging, running off-tackle plays, over and over. Seeing me standing on the sidelines, Meadows wandered over and said without preamble, "I just got me a couple of new rabbit dogs. Want to see 'em?" "Sure," I said, figuring that he meant we'd go see them after practice. Instead, he waved to his No. 1 assistant coach, Larrie Robinson, and said: "We're going over to the house. Go ahead with practice." We drove across town, and he spent the better part of an hour, on the week of his biggest game of the year, showing off his two new beagles, tugging on their long floppy ears and bragging about what great hunting dogs they were destined to become. As soon as we returned to practice, Meadows strolled over to Robinson and said, "OK, take 'em on in." Two nights later, Butler beat previously undefeated Huntsville. I later asked Meadows, "Why did you leave practice that day the week of the Huntsville game?" "They didn't need me there," he replied with a grin. "I could tell on Tuesday they were ready to play."

"John was a little different sometimes," said former Lee High coach Keith Wilson, another of Meadows' main rivals in the '60s and '70s. "But you could always count on one thing. You had to get lucky because you weren't going to out-coach him." Usually, you weren't going to out-motivate him either.

Several years ago, many of his former players, coaches, and friends honored Tom Owen during a Huntsville High School football reunion at Huntsville Country Club. Among those invited were Keith Wilson and John Meadows. Former Huntsville player Chuck Cooper, who became a prominent lawyer in Washington, D.C., recalled the 1969 Huntsville-Butler game, which the Panthers won in an upset. "After the game, Coach Owen was asked how we were able to win," Cooper said. "His answer was succinct: 'We're Huntsville and they're Butler.'" Nobody enjoyed the story more than Meadows who was patiently waiting in the wings to describe his own views of the supercharged Butler-Huntsville rivalry. Owen always hyped the notion that whenever you put on that red jersey, you were different, you were special, you were supposed to win. Across town on the other side of the tracks, Meadows was using the same sort of psychology—in reverse. Pointing good-naturedly to Owen, Meadows said, "If we were from Butler, we didn't know how to read or write, according to him. That's what I'd tell my players anyway. I'd say, 'They're over there looking down their noses, saying you wear white socks to church on Sunday, saying they're better than you are, thinking they're better than you are. What are you going to do about it?'" Tom Owen laughed along with everybody else. Recalling the occasion years later, Owen chuckled and said, "John Meadows didn't miss many tricks." Indeed, he didn't. Yes, he always went back to the basics when it came to football. But as the subtitle of this book suggests, there's a lot more to winning than X's and O's.

John Pruett,
Sports Editor
The Huntsville Times

FOREWORD

The first time I met Coach John Meadows was at a baseball game at St. Bernard College in the spring of 1955. The game was between St. Bernard Prep School and Hanceville High School. I was having a conversation with my old friend Allen Green who was playing for Hanceville that day.

Coach Meadows joined us, and I remember his asking Allen several questions about the upcoming Hanceville football team and what he thought about their prospects of beating Cullman that year. At that time Coach Meadows was an assistant football coach at Cullman High School. As he talked I didn't think that much about the tenor of his questions and passed it off as a coach trying to get a feel for his competition. But in retrospect, it seemed prophetic since Coach Meadows had not yet officially been contacted about the head coach's job at Hanceville. Subsequently, he was offered and accepted the Hanceville job and beat Cullman 7–0 in the 1955 football season, his first year as a head coach.

In the last few years, I have gotten to know Coach Meadows primarily through his continued close relationship with the 1955 and 1956 Hanceville football teams that he coached. Even a casual observer could look at the records of those two teams and conclude that they had received outstanding coaching. What the statistical records would not show, however, is that coaching was only part of the good fortune that these players received by being mentored by such an outstanding man. He taught them about becoming responsible men and being good citizens—qualities that have continued to serve them well to this day. After more than fifty years, Coach Meadows still comes to all of their reunions and many of the Bulldog Coffee Club meetings that are regularly held at Hanceville.

He coached at several other high schools during his lengthy career, including Gordo, Scottsboro, Butler of Huntsville, and Lincoln County, Tennessee, and success followed him everywhere he went.

In a recent conversation with Coach Meadows, he revealed one of his winning strategies. He said that he sometimes picked out the opponent's best and toughest player and had his best player or players dominate him the entire game. He rightly observed, with the corners of his mouth turning in that affirmative smile he has, "There's nothing more discouraging to a football team than having their best player getting his butt whipped on every play."

Even after his retirement from coaching, he continues to volunteer his time and expertise to assist area coaches with their teams. After his 80th birthday, Coach Meadows assisted Lee High School in Huntsville, Alabama, in attaining city championships and state playoff berths. At the present time he is working with the football team and coaches at Giles County High School in Tennessee.

I have had the pleasure of teaching some of his former players, and it's very noticeable that when Coach Meadows' name is mentioned, the conversation always turns from football and is centered on what he has taught them about life.

To his former players, fans, and those who appreciate the fine art of coaching football and developing leaders, he has become an icon, a figure bigger than life. For many years the teams he coached were always dreaded opponents for the coaches in both Alabama and Tennessee. We all are indeed fortunate that Coach Meadows has written this book so that just a small part of what he knows about football and living life will be preserved in perpetuity. It is unlikely that we will again see a man who has contributed more to Alabama and Tennessee high school football and to the molding of good citizens than has Coach John Meadows.

Edward Ward, Ph.D.
U.S. Air Force Colonel, Retired
Microbiology Professor, Alabama A & M University, Retired
Avid Hanceville High School Supporter

About the Author

John Louie Meadows was born in Neel, Alabama, a place so small that you don't bother looking for a dot representing it on any map. Although this is his given name and the one that you would find on a certificate stored somewhere in an ancient filing cabinet in the Morgan County Courthouse, the hundreds of athletes and coaches who have had the honor of the life-changing experience of just being around him for even a short time all call him—"Coach." In the field of coaching, a man's success is usually defined by the number of wins and losses attached to his résumé. Of course, this is true of this coaching legend in two states, Alabama and Tennessee, but records and statistics can't begin to describe the achievements of someone like Coach Meadows. One of his outstanding players is quoted as saying, "Coach Meadows' record speaks for itself, but his ability to take average and below-average athletes and instill in them the confidence and desire to become overachievers while teaching them to win and perform with class is unparalleled."

Now let me speak about that résumé and the accomplishments found within its pages. There is only a handful of coaches who have ever walked the sidelines who can match it and even fewer who can boast of one better. John Meadows began his coaching career in Cullman, Alabama, as an assistant under Grady Elmore in 1952 and 1953 and Homer Wesley in 1954. After three years at Cullman, Meadows was hired as the head coach at Hanceville, Alabama, located only ten miles away and a staunch rival of Cullman at the time. His first year as a head coach proved to be the standard that would characterize his illustrious career. His 1955 Hanceville team was undefeated and won the state title, having only one touchdown scored on them all year. After only a two-year stay at Hanceville, with a record of 17–2–1, Coach Meadows left Hanceville and took the head job in the small Alabama town of Gordo. There he continued his winning ways. Meadows' 1957 team was also undefeated, and the '58 team tasted defeat only one time, leaving him with a two-year record of 16–1–2. In 1959 Coach Meadows returned to North Alabama, answering the call of Scottsboro High School. In seven years his teams went undefeated twice, sporting a 10–0 record in both 1960 and 1965. The 1960 team finished second in the state, and the 1965 team was declared state champions. Following the state-championship year, tradition-rich S.R. Butler High School in Huntsville, Alabama, called, and he answered, giving the Rebels an undefeated season his second year there. While at Butler, his team was selected by a poll of sportswriters and coaches from all over the state as the "Best-Prepared Team in Alabama." During his thirteen years at Butler, Coach Meadows amassed 92 more victories with 33 defeats and 1 tie.

After thirty years of coaching in the state of Alabama at four different schools where he had produced at least one undefeated team at each school, two state championships, and a reputation revered by all who knew him, Coach Meadows retired from Alabama and took on the challenge of a newly consolidated school just across the Alabama-Tennessee line. Lincoln County High School in Fayetteville, Tennessee, was formed when five small rival schools were combined into one large one. A special person was needed to fuse together a community that suddenly merged into one school so many students who had been bitter enemies on the athletic fields for so many years. That special person was Coach John Meadows. In only his fourth year at the new school, his 1982 Falcons won the Tennessee State Championship. His 1984 team went 10–0 in the regular season and was not scored on until the ninth ball game, which they won 49–6. This team received national recognition, being ranked in the top twenty-five for most of the season. After ten years as the head man at Lincoln County, Coach Meadows' record was 87 wins, 27 defeats, and 6 ties. Through thirty-four years as a head coach at five different schools in two different states, Coach Meadows' record is 271–76–7, which averages to be almost eight victories per year. If questioned about his outstanding record, Coach Meadows invariably responds with a humble statement such as this: "I didn't have all that much to do with it. I always had the support of great administrators, great assistant coaches, and the backing of an appreciative community. These are the people who deserve the praise. I just hung around and watched."

Phenomenal accomplishments such as these in athletics are *not* the norm, and those in that field have recognized this in the career of Coach John Meadows. Of this coaching legend, John Pruett, the longtime sports editor of *The Huntsville Times* wrote: "In all the years of covering sports for *The Huntsville Times*, I don't believe I've ever seen a finer high school coach than John Meadows." These sentiments have been echoed through the years by his peers and associates as witnessed by the following list of honors:

COACH-OF-THE-YEAR AWARDS:

- **Alabama State Coach of the Year—1955, 1957, 1960, 1965, 1967**
- **Tennessee State Coach of the Year—1982, 1984**
- **Tri-State (Alabama, Tennessee, Georgia) Coach of the Year—1960**

HALL-OF-FAME INDUCTIONS:

- **Jacksonville State University Gamecock Hall of Fame—1985**
- **Huntsville-Madison County Athletic Hall of Fame—1989**
- **Alabama High School Sports Hall of Fame—1993**
- **Morgan County Sports Hall of Fame—1994**
- **Pickens County Sports Hall of Fame—1995**
- **Cullman County Sports Hall of Fame—2004**

In addition to his hall-of-fame induction, Coach Meadows' accomplishments while playing for Jacksonville State University were rewarded by Little All-American honors in 1949. He was selected as a member of JSU's Centennial Team, representing the top 100 athletes from 1883–1983, and he was the Alumnus of the Year for his alma mater in 1969.

After his second *official* retirement from a career dedicated to winning games in football and producing winners in the game of life, Coach Meadows is still very much involved in the coaching field, assisting anyone who is lucky enough to have his phone number. I can't bring to mind anyone who is better qualified to author a book directed to a profession of which he has been such a stellar member for over half a century than is this slow-talking, fast-thinking country boy from Neel, Alabama—John Louie Meadows.

Doug Styles
Assistant Coach for Coach John Meadows
1964–1978

PREFACE

My association with the game of football began in the small North Alabama town of Falkville, located on Highway 31, which was at the time the main road from Birmingham to Nashville. When I was ten years old, my father was killed by a drunk driver while he and I were walking up the road about half a mile apart. In addition to my mother, I had three younger brothers and a sister, and the times that were hard before this tragedy suddenly became much harder. When one is faced with a situation of this nature, he can either crawl into a shell and feel sorry for himself, or he can face the realization and become a competitor in this game we call life. When faced with the consequence that at the age of ten, fate had suddenly thrust me into the position of the *man of the family,* I chose the latter, and competition has been the motivation that has kept my wheels turning all of my life. In high school I not only competed in all sports, but I also competed in the classroom and was the valedictorian of the senior class of 1942. Upon graduation I joined the United States Army Air Forces where they discovered and used my athletic skills in football and baseball. Following my stint in the military, I ended up back in Alabama at Jacksonville State University where I continued my pursuit of competition on the football team as a receiver and defensive back. With this brief background, one can better understand my selected lifelong occupation as a teacher and coach. I have always aspired to transfer to others my desire to compete and excel, especially to the younger generation, and what better way to do this than as a mentor on the field of competition. I have always believed the old adage that "Success is attained when desire is combined with dedication and hard work." I have enjoyed this success in my life, not only on the athletic field but also with my family and with the many friends I have gained through the past seven decades following that calamitous event on Highway 31. This brings me to the reason for this book. These friends and my family have exhorted me for years to capture on paper an account of the reasons for this success. So what follows is a tangible resource that will hopefully guide and assist those who read it to also experience that special feeling one gets as he overcomes the obstacles in his life—whether they be tragic personal ones or merely the next scheduled ball game.

The title itself, *BACK TO THE BASICS: Winning Is More Than X's and O's,* is an indication of its contents. I wanted to produce a book that isn't just a compilation of football plays and defensive alignments but, along with these necessary components of the game, have in it what has been the basic philosophy that I have used in developing a winning program. Throughout the pages I have given my perspective on the various aspects of the game of football from the initial arrival in the community where your team is located to the preparation needed for the championship game. Through the past fifty-plus years, I have influenced and been influenced by several hundred players, coaches, and many others associated with my chosen profession. I have, ingrained in the depths of my mind, many stories concerning this horde of humanity who has been the whole of my professional existence for so many years. I have intentionally not mentioned anyone's name in any of the anecdotal accounts that I have used to illustrate many of the various factors involved in a championship football program. The reason for this omission is not that I don't remember those names, but with so many special people involved, I don't want to inadvertently leave anyone out.

It is my sincere desire that those who read this book will find within its pages at least one small thing that will make them better equipped to compete—not only as coaches but as individuals devoted to being examples to all of the young men and women whom they may have the privilege and responsibility of influencing—to instill in *their* lives that intangible quality of competition that will guide *them* into being *winners* in whatever endeavors *they* might pursue.

Coach John Louie Meadows

ACKNOWLEDGMENTS

The publication of this book could not have been possible without the assistance and encouragement of too many people for me to list individually. As is true with any publication involving the football coaching profession, there are excerpts for which I cannot claim originality. Through over fifty years of note taking at scores of coaching clinics around the country, I have compiled ideas from countless coaches whose names I don't even remember but to whom I remain most thankful. For any success that I have enjoyed that may have been responsible for the prompting of this book, I humbly express my gratitude to all of the supportive administrators, co-workers, excellent and dedicated assistants, loyal members of each community, and all of the committed athletes and their parents who made it all possible.

I express special appreciation to Doug Styles, a faithful assistant and devoted friend, for helping me convey my thoughts and ideas in written form through this book. I am also indebted to his wife, Nancy, my eighth grade science student and our babysitter fifty-five years ago, for the hours that she spent editing the contents. I must also extend my sincere thanks to Doug and Nancy's three sons, Bryan, Dan, and Clay Styles, all excellent football coaches in their own rights, for their contributions to this publication. For the section on various blocking schemes used with the Zone Offense, I extend my gratitude to Coach David Smothers.

I am most grateful for the introduction submitted by John Pruett, Sports Editor of *The Huntsville Times* and a longtime friend, and for the foreword by Ed Ward, a friend and supporter for many years.

Particular appreciation must be given to my son, John Blake Meadows, and to his wife, Malissa, for their technical assistance in the formatting and publishing of this book. I also give a loving thank-you to my three daughters, Judy, Beth, and Jane, for their encouragement and constant support shown to me all of their lives. Finally—and most of all—I thank my steady companion and wonderful wife, Glenda, who has patiently shared almost six decades of living with this old coach.

John L. Meadows

PART I

ESSENTIAL ELEMENTS IN DEVELOPING A CHAMPIONSHIP PROGRAM

Chapter 1

Creating an Atmosphere in a Community That Expects To Win Because Of You and Your Program

Selling Your Program

When you, as a coach, move into a community, whether it is in a one-school small town or in a large city with several schools, you have a product to sell. The product is you and your football program. Not only do you have to sell the players themselves, but you have to sell the entire community—including the parents and the school administration and staff who *all* must be convinced that we aren't there just to win football games but to instill academic, social, and moral values as well. Successful teams thrive in a positive, competitive atmosphere and can never reach their potential when either one of these groups is not totally sold on your program.

In high school we are told that we can't recruit our players. True, you aren't supposed to entice studs from all over the region to attend your school, but there are no rules that say we can't recruit our own school and our own community. I have produced winning programs in five different schools in five different communities and two states, and through the years, I have learned that when you declare yourself "a coach," you're going to be overworked, underpaid, and second-guessed. Coaching a football team is somewhat like running a Wal-Mart store—it's 24/7/365. When I moved into a community, I wanted to make sure that every eligible male student (or potential student) knew the face of John Meadows. Anywhere they rolled out a ball, swung a bat, or just met to shoot the bull, I tried to be there and tell them how good they would look in purple and gold, black and gold, green and gold, red and blue, or whatever colors the local team donned on Friday night. I realized that not only was I recruiting the players, but I had to sell the parents as well. When I found out where Mama and Daddy hung out, I'd also be there selling "Old John" and his football program.

Another group of very special people who have to be sold on your product is your co-workers—the teachers and administration at your school. These are the folks who can make you or break you in the eyes of the public, the parents, and especially the players. These are the people who project your image and your team's image at church, in the Elks Club, or even in the grocery line at Piggly Wiggly. Teachers are an invaluable factor in your program, and as coaches, we must make sure that those young men who wear our colors are never a liability but always an asset in their classrooms.

Most of our players are as motivated in the classroom as on the field, but there are a few who need a little goading when it comes to the academic aspect of success in high school. Also, there are many students who go home to a one-parent home and receive little or no encouragement or assistance with homework or other school-related problems. Coaches need to recognize this from the beginning and have a plan of early involvement that includes a constant monitoring of the athletes' grades and classroom behavior. This is a big reason why we need to establish a good working relationship with our co-workers. I firmly believe that the coaches in a school should be the most visible, friendly, and helpful members on the staff. I realize that there are stressful moments in all fields of teaching, but classroom teachers should remember that when they give a test, the only ones who know the score are the students, the teacher, and maybe the parents. On the other hand, when coaches "give *their* tests," 8,000 people watch, and thousands more read about the outcome in the morning paper. As teachers are convinced that our goals are the same—to develop and produce outstanding members of our community—they are usually eager to inform us of a less-than-stellar performance by one of ours before it's too late. One tool that has proven to be effective is a peer-tutoring program. With the assistance of their teachers, outstanding students in each course are recommended to tutor the academically deficient athlete and to assist with difficult assignments. We set a time, usually an hour before school, when the tutor and the athlete (or athletes) meet to go over homework, review for tests, or clear up any problems that may surface. Here again, teachers who recognize our common interest in our students are pleased to support this program. The booster club is usually excited to sponsor this program, and for their time, the tutors are rewarded with a little spending money.

I have observed, through over fifty years of association with athletes, that the influence the coach has over their young minds usually exceeds that of other teachers, friends, and even family. If the selling job on the athletes is genuine and complete, their display of attitude and interest in succeeding both in school and on the playing field will convince the other participants of this successful program that what you have to offer is well worth their time and energy. When the product (you and your program) is sold and the machine is running well, although it will need "greasing" from time to time, the final result is a group of disciplined, productive members of society who just happen to be a squad of aggressive young men who know how to win—in life as well as on the gridiron.

Providing the Best Instruction Possible on the Football Field

If we expect our players to be exemplary role models in the classroom and before their peers, we can ask nothing less of our coaches. Coaches should honestly attempt to be beyond reproach, realizing that any negative thing they do will be a reflection of the entire team and program. One careless act of misconduct can destroy months and years of developing positive school and community support necessary for a successful program. In order for a program to be successful, every staff member must be loyal to the administration and devoted to work within the policies of the system. They must strive to develop and maintain not only the skills and knowledge needed to teach the latest football techniques but also the traits exemplified in all stellar members of the community in which they perform. Through many years in this profession, I've found that the students who suit up and represent their schools every Friday night may be hard-pressed to name the English teacher who made them read *A Tale of Two Cities* but can give you the name of every coach on the staff. Impressions we make on these young men are indelible and often life changing, and we better make sure that they are positive and not negative.

Familiarizing Your Coaches with Every Phase of the Game and Encouraging Them in Developing an Inquisitive Mind and a Total Dedication to the Game

Although each coach has specific and general coaching duties, the entire staff should be familiar with every phase of the game. Don't be so proud that you can't (or won't) learn from other coaches. I've learned things from ninth grade coaches that have helped me to be a better coach. It has always been my contention that teachers can learn from this facet of the coaching game. Good coaches are the biggest copycats in the world. If Coach Jones is winning more football games than I am, with the same type personnel, I'm going to visit Coach Jones and find out why. If I teach English and Mrs. Jones's English students, with the same English background, are scoring higher on the standardized test than *my* students, I should swallow my pride and visit Mrs. Jones's classroom. Because football is constantly changing, coaches must work together in order to stay up with the latest advances on both sides of the ball. A coach who is assigned specific offensive duties can't perform those duties with the proficiency and confidence that he must have unless he understands the various aspects of the defenses that he'll be facing. The same is true of the defensive coaches and their understanding of the offensive techniques and strategies that they'll be defending.

Developing and Displaying a Positive, Outgoing Attitude Necessary in Recognizing the Potential That Lies Within Those We Coach

As mentioned, coaches must be loyal to the school, but most of all, they *must* be loyal to the head coach. Any negative comments should be kept in-house and solved before the start of each practice. Dissention is easily recognized by our players and does nothing but plant seeds of doubt in their minds about the entire program. To attain the common goal, which includes all the aspects of winning that I've already discussed, teamwork among the coaches is imperative if we are to realize the success desired. Just because I'm a defensive coach, I should not be afraid to point out an error made by an offensive player that went unnoticed by the coaches who have the responsibility for that side of the game. With this said, there is still the important duty that rests with *you* as the head coach to place your coaches in positions in which they can best help your team.

Assigning Coaching Duties According To Their Knowledge, Abilities, and Experience

Assignments will depend upon the size of your program and the number of coaches available—the bigger the program, the more coaches and therefore the more specialized assignments. Many things in this life are learned by trial and error. The problem with that philosophy in the game of football is that they put your "errors" in your record book and on the sports page of the local newspaper for the entire community to see. Often, depending once again on the size of your program, your assistants may not be seasoned veteran coaches, but regardless of their knowledge and experience, it is still up to *you* to "coach the coaches" as you install *your* brand of football. After you have done this, it is imperative that you <u>let them coach!</u> Too often through the years, I have observed that very good coaches may hire and train highly qualified assistants, but then they try to do all the coaching themselves. Not only is this very tiring and time-consuming for you, but it is also very frustrating for the young or inexperienced—and especially for the veteran coach. This frustration is quickly passed on to the players, and consequently we as a staff are guilty of not providing our best instruction on the field—and the result is usually more L's than W's broadcast in that local paper.

Involving Active and Positive Members of the Community in Your Program

The development of a championship program has a great deal to do with the *reason* you were hired. If the primary reason that you are there is because the boosters felt that their program needed *just* a coaching change, don't unpack the truck! A big "heads up" along these lines is the conversations that you hear from these boosters prior to and even during your interview. I don't like to hear these people criticize other coaches unless they are saying, "We've hired him seven or eight good assistants, built him a quarter-million-dollar field house with a state-of-the-art weight room and all these other things—and our program is still not improving—WHY?" When you move into a new job, remember these three very important rules: define the problem, confine the problem, and then attack the problem! It must be pointed out to these folks that they need to visit the schools on our schedule *with good programs* and check the number of coaches that *they* have, *their* facilities and *their* equipment, and compare *them* to what they are asking *their own* coaches to win with.

About thirty years ago, along with several other successful high school coaches, I was privileged to speak at a coaching clinic in Georgia. One of these coaches who spoke was Nick Hyder from Valdosta, Georgia, who is said by many to be the best high school coach ever in that state. In a twenty-two-year period, Coach Hyder won 249 games, including seven state championships and three national championships. I think that it is safe to say that his *was* a very successful high school program. In his presentation and also in my personal conversations with Coach Hyder, he disclosed what he considered to be the secret of his great success: "First of all, I've had great assistant coaches. When I have a coaches' meeting, there are twenty-one guys present. This sounds like a big number, but you need to realize that not only does this include my varsity staff but all the way down to the sixth grade team. Every football team in Valdosta runs the same offense and the same defense, using the same terminology consistent with *my* philosophy and program. If the sixth grade team runs Sweep Right, I know that they are calling it and running it the same way the varsity Wildcats do on Friday night. It also goes without saying that I've had great players. Valdosta, Georgia, is a *football* town. When you drive through most towns, in every backyard where a male child lives, you see a basketball goal—not in Valdosta. In most backyards here in this town, the kids have a goal post erected. It has never been difficult to entice the good athletes to participate in our program. Not only do we teach our young men how to play football, but even more importantly, we teach them respect—respect for their parents, for their teachers, for their coaches, for their opponents, and most of all, respect for themselves." I have never forgotten these words of wisdom from this coaching legend and believe that all of the things he mentioned are equally important if a program is to reach its full potential.

Soliciting and Earning the Confidence and Support of Administration, Staff, and Students

Successful programs must not only have the support of the community but also of the administration, the staff, and the entire student body of the school. The successful program cannot exist without the backing of your principal and the teachers who have been convinced that your program will make the entire school and community better in all respects. Several years ago, I accepted a job at a school that had at one time enjoyed success but due to several factors had recently fallen on hard times. I was promised the complete backing of an administration who realized that a winning football program would enhance the image and performance of the entire school. This team had a record of 0–9–1 the previous season, and the JV team of the school I was leaving had beaten their returning players 24–0 in a late-season contest. I accepted the position because of their rich tradition and because of the genuine concern displayed by the administration—and because I believed that I could win football games there. The first request that I made was to hire a coaching staff of my choosing, which was granted. I was also told that a new school was in the plans, which made the job more enticing. The backing of the principal was proven the first few days of spring training. We called a practice on Saturday morning to have a routine two-hour scrimmage. About half way through practice, it started to rain, and we retreated to the gym to finish with some one-on-one in our tennis shoes on some tumbling mats I found in the girls' storage closet. I'll admit that we stayed in the rain long enough to become "slightly" muddy which quickly transferred from our uniforms to the mats. After we were finished, I instructed the managers to clean up the mats and to put them back in the closet. When I arrived at school on Monday morning, it was evident that the managers' idea of clean and that of the lady P.E. teacher were slightly different. She greeted me in the gym with her hands on her hips and fire in her eyes. I listened patiently as she told me in no uncertain terms how she felt about my borrowing her tumbling mats. After what seemed to be her final disgruntled remark, "What makes you think that you can come in here and tear up my mats without even asking me?" she stormed off to inform the principal what a no-good he had hired as a football coach. I felt compelled to reply, and in my most humble and matter-of-fact voice, I told her, "Lady, you can also tell him that I'm sorry about your mats and that I'll buy you some new ones, but let me promise you this: Before I leave here, I'm gonna tear up a lot of things!" Her trip to the office *did* produce a visit to the gym by the principal whose response solidified the support I had been promised. Upon his arrival he asked me, "How was practice Saturday, John?" "Wet!" I replied, expecting some sort of reprimand. "Don't worry about those tumbling mats. I told her that we'd get her some new ones. You keep those. I'm sure you'll need them again sometime." With that he turned and walked away. I made a vow right then that I would not let that gentleman down. We *would* have a winning football team. I also realized that I needed that strong-willed P.E. teacher on my side. The following morning, our first meeting in the gym was somewhat different from the previous one. I presented her with a big red rose and a very humble and sincere apology. She was a very fine and gracious lady, and this mat incident was the starting point of an excellent working relationship and a lasting friendship.

Developing the Team Through Off-Season Duties and Responsibilities

It has always been my conviction that most football games are *won* or *lost* from January to August and that the ten or fifteen-week schedule posted on your dressing- room wall is just where you add the scores. The things that you, your coaches, and the players do throughout these eight months to develop the *team* that you display on Friday night during those other four or five months are usually the difference in which side of the column the bigger number goes on. Neither a coach nor a team can remain successful if they become satisfied with what they have accomplished. I believe that as a coach you have the duty and responsibility to constantly look for new techniques and ideas to make your program better. I can't count the number of football clinics that I've attended throughout the country in the past fifty-five years. I've listened to and taken notes from some of the most successful coaches to ever walk the sidelines—John McKay, Bo Schembechler, Lou Holtz, Woody Hayes, Eddie Robinson, Bobby Bowden, Joe Paterno, "Shug" Jordan, Bud Wilkinson, Paul "Bear" Bryant—and the list could go on and on. Although I did pick up some great ideas from these hall-of-fame coaches, I found that you usually learn more from other coaches who are in the same boat you are. Most of what I learned at these clinics was the result of all-night sessions of swapping ideas and stealing ideas that have been tried and tested by the old coach who has to win with what the mamas and daddies give him, not with what he can recruit from all over the country. Many things that you take home from these clinics can't be recorded in a notebook. While discussing the problems that other coaches confront in dealing with the sixteen and seventeen-year-old hormone-infested young men who have your job in their hands every Friday night, I have found that they are very similar to those I contended with on a daily basis. Dealing with girlfriends, too much homework, hard exams, family problems, and an excess of other earth-shattering tribulations usually place the coach and next week's opponent far down the list of priorities. Success demands that the coaches get involved to a certain degree in the home life of *all* their players.

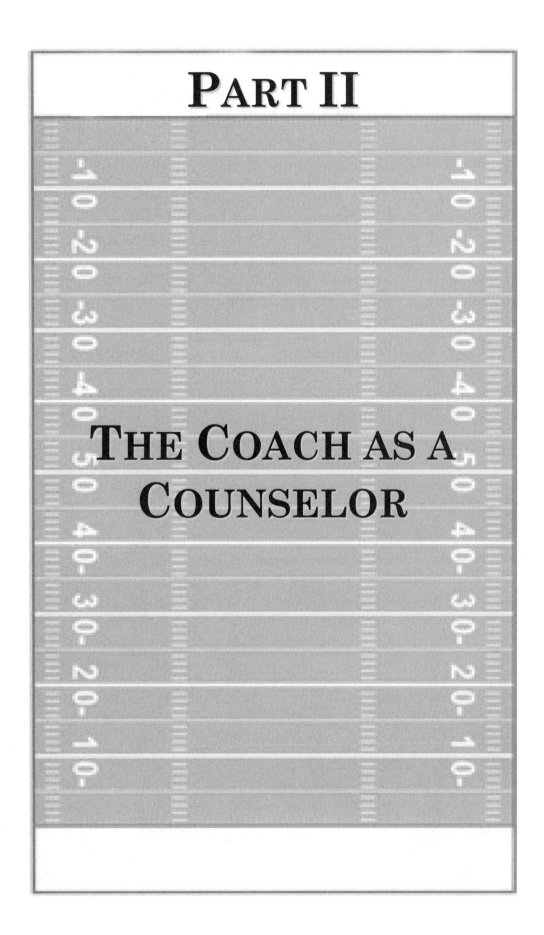

PART II

THE COACH AS A COUNSELOR

Chapter 2

Coaching Responsibilities That Do Not Involve Football

Defining the Coach

When one goes to the dictionary and looks up the word *coach*, the following synonyms are given: teacher, trainer, instructor. Certainly all of these terms are applicable to a line of work that involves filling a pliable young mind with a complicated set of instructions to be fulfilled while someone lined up on the other side of the ball is trying to sidetrack him while inflicting bodily harm with what he too has been taught. Over the past half-century, I have seen the evolution of numerous offensive and defensive philosophies that, when implemented correctly, have produced many victories. Too often, coaches place too much confidence in these "instructions" represented by X's and O's and neglect a most important and definitely more difficult aspect of our profession—dealing with the individual problems involved in being a teenager. Later, I will talk about goals and goal setting and the importance of the dedicated effort of every team member to attain these realistic objectives.

Addressing Individual Problems of the Teenager

What every coach must realize is that the success of your program lies in the ability of these sixteen and seventeen-year-old young men to remain focused on these goals and still contend with the individual and unique problems associated with adolescence. Many years ago, I was asked to address this subject at a coaching clinic where I discussed how, through the years, I had dealt with the following situations involving my team members:

1. Family problems
2. Social problems
3. Financial problems
4. Psychological problems
5. School problems

1. Family Problems

When you deal with fifty to one hundred young men each year, it doesn't take you long to realize that not all of them are being reared by the Cleavers or the Nelsons. Most of the parents that I've dealt with have been very supportive of our football program and our coaches, but there have been times that a heartfelt talk with certain parents was needed to solidify their support, which made a big difference in how we coached their kids. I can bring to mind many situations through the years when a player was not giving me or the team one hundred percent effort. Before bringing the house down on the erring athlete, I would have a nice, friendly talk with the parents and convince them that I was going to be their top assistant in rearing Little Johnny and that all he needed was a little hard work to mold him into the model child. If handled properly, this parent-coach conference will ward off any negative feedback from the parents when their child comes home complaining about the hard work you're having him to do. Rather, when they go home and declare the old coach mean and overbearing and unfair, the parents will be quick to give you support and readily convince him that what you are doing is for his own good.

I must admit that there have been times when a player has disappointed me and slipped through the cracks in spite of all that I could do to help him. But I am thankful to say that the success stories far exceed the disappointments. One in particular is worth the telling.

At the beginning of fall practice one year, a starting receiver and defensive back came to me and very reluctantly told me that he would not be able to practice on Thursday. I realized that for this fellow to miss practice, he must have a really good reason, so I told him that missing one practice wouldn't hurt him and that he could easily catch up. "You don't understand, Coach. I mean *every* Thursday." I'm sure that on that set of regulations posted on someone else's dressing-room wall, there was a rule that would have terminated this young man's career. I pulled him aside and asked him a three-word question: "What's the problem?" He answered, "Coach, I'm the only one at home who has a license. My grandmother gets her check on Thursday, and I have to take her to buy groceries." I trusted his integrity and said that it would be fine for him to miss and not to worry about it. Further investigation revealed that indeed he *was* the only one with a license—the only one of the *twelve* who were being reared by this eighty-seven-year-old marvelous lady in a three-room house behind the dog pound. I *did* receive some static from other coaches and even some booster daddies who questioned that decision and how it would affect the rest of the team. However, the only consequence this situation had on the team was a positive one. If you are effectively doing that selling job I talked about, your team is *sold* on *everything* you ask them to do. This positive attitude develops the camaraderie and dependence on each other necessary to be successful in *any* endeavor—especially a winning football program. As Paul Harvey says in his radio show, "Now...for the rest of the story!" Of the twelve children being reared by this saintly grandmother, in what were much less than ideal conditions, there were three brothers who played football for me. All three received college scholarships, and all three graduated from college and are now very successful, productive members of the community in which they live.

Still another aspect of the coaching profession that has nothing to do with reading the option or jacking someone's jaw on defense is understanding that the personalities and social problems of every player on the squad, from the all-state quarterback to the third-string field-goal kicker, will differ and demand special and diverse attention. I have discussed team discipline with other coaches who post a list of rigid rules that, if invoked when I was a player, would have placed me in the end-zone bleachers on Friday night. The first thing that I teach a young assistant is that we *are* going to have discipline, but we can't discipline them if they're pulling out of the school parking lot at three o'clock looking for trouble. I mentioned their parents, but as their coaches, we must remember that for some of these kids, *we* are all that they have—and if they aren't out there, we can't help them. This philosophy is pretty easy to adhere to when the stud that is averaging 180 yards a game messes up, but it is just as true for those who need *us* a whole lot more than we need *them*.

2. Social Problems—Football: The Great Equalizer

From time to time I have been asked to speak at various churches in the community where I was coaching. Usually, I started each speech with the following statement: "Most of you know who I am. I'm John Meadows, and I coach football. I'm here to declare to you tonight that football is sometimes better than the church." If you think *that* statement won't turn some heads and open some eyes down at your local congregation—try it sometime! Before the members could locate their rail to ride me out on, I was always quick to follow that supposedly blasphemous statement with my humble explanation. I would hurriedly remind them of what the earthly brother of our Lord said in James Chapter 2: *[1]My brethren, do not hold your faith in our glorious Lord Jesus Christ with an attitude of personal favoritism. [2]For if a man comes into your assembly with a gold ring and dressed in fine clothes, and there also comes in a poor man in dirty clothes, [3]and you pay special attention to the one who is wearing the fine clothes, and say, "You sit here in a good place," and you say to the poor man, "You stand over there, or sit down by my footstool," [4]have you not made distinctions among yourselves, and become judges with evil motives?* James 2:1–4.

My love for football began at an early age in Falkville, Alabama, a very small town a few miles south of Decatur. I was the second man James describes in Verse 2. Although my clothes weren't dirty, they were old and had been broken in by whoever handed them down to me. I was never ashamed of who I was, but I'm sure that those faded blue overalls sported in my senior picture in the Falkville annual of 1942 *did* cause a few to make "*distinctions among [themselves].*" But every Friday night during my high school career, when I slipped on that Blue Devil uniform and caught touchdown passes, I was accepted by *all* my classmates and by *all* who were in the stands, from the richest to the poorest. Football eliminates the class system in our society like nothing else. There is no place for "*personal favoritism*" on the football field. I certainly received a great deal of *personal satisfaction* from every one of my victories but not nearly as much as I did from seeing those kids who lined up for me, those who came from the projects and from the three-room shack down by the dog pound, being accepted by the community as much as the banker's son. What a feeling of fulfillment it is to look up in the bleachers on the fifty-yard line and see the quarterback's dad and the right guard's dad—one black and one white—high-fiving each other after an important score. Seeing that man dressed in fine clothes with the big gold ring sitting by the factory worker dressed in the dirty work clothes he had to hurry from work in so he wouldn't miss the opening kickoff also made my chest swell with pride. No, football is *not* better than the church, but sometimes it *can* help the entire community accomplish this admonition of unity and humility given by James to his brethren.

3. Financial Problems

One of the most difficult things that many young coaches must come to grips with is the fact that our players have a life away from the football field. Along with the family and social problems facing many of our players, we must realize that for some it is necessary that they contribute to the family income. Almost every year that I coached, I had to contend with one or more players who *had* to maintain a part-time job. A set of rigid rules, in lieu of common sense and a little compassion, would have terminated the football career of many good athletes. In these situations it is important that the coach have a good relationship with the leaders of the community, some of whom hopefully are also leaders of your booster club. I have always managed to work my football practice schedule around a player's part-time job provided by an interested employer willing to provide a flexible work schedule for the industrious athlete. It has also been my experience that the majority of these young men not only displayed exemplary work ethics on these part-time jobs but also on the field of play and in the classroom. The example of such a young man who sticks in my mind was a senior player whose father was dead and whose mother and two younger siblings struggled to survive on her meager salary in a very modest little house not three blocks from the school. A staunch booster, who knew the family and who had coached this fellow in peewee football, explained the situation to me and also told me that he had helped him get a job at a local supermarket that was also located three blocks from the school. I promise you that the fact that this wiry athlete was one of the best blocking backs that I have ever coached was *not* a contributing factor in my releasing him from practice every day forty-five minutes early so that he could put in a good five hours helping his family make ends meet. I would have provided—and in fact did provide on other occasions—the same opportunity for players who played only when we were way ahead or way behind. Much of our practice time after we released this young man was spent on conditioning, but this facet of his game was never in jeopardy. He was always first on the field running on his own, and during our drills and scrimmages or in the games, he never showed any sign of fatigue. Not only did this remarkable youngster excel in football, destroying linebackers and defensive ends in our power attack, but he also excelled in track the following spring, competing in the 440-yard run. One of my assistants, who was also the head track coach, had made similar arrangements for him to maintain his work schedule right through track season. Because of his work schedule, he was forced to miss several meets, but at those held during the times he could compete, the 440 usually belonged to him. There was one time during his career when he asked his boss for time off—for the city track meet held on a Saturday. This meet had special meaning for him since the 440 man from a rival city school was one of the few who had crossed the finish line before him during the meets in which he had competed. As the announcer made the last call for the 440-yard run, I was standing by my assistant as he shook his head and said, "I don't know about this. He didn't practice all week so that he could work extra to make up for today." "He'll do fine," I assured him. The 440 is a grueling *gut-check*—a sprint one time around the track in which rigorous training is required to compete successfully. The key words in that statement are *gut-check*: a coaching term that describes a situation in which the involved athlete must perform above his normal capability. Standing near the finish line, my assistant and I were directly across from the halfway point in this arduous event. At that point our inspiring performer was a good twenty yards behind his cross-town competitor—and things were looking bad. The last 220 yards of that race brought tears to my eyes and caused my chest to swell with pride as our determined young stud looked like a fighter jet that had just turned on the after-burners. Not only did he evaporate that twenty-yard lead, but he established one of his own as he broke the tape with that same lead over his astonished opponent. It was the following Monday during our morning break that we learned the story behind this fantastic accomplishment of the preceding Saturday. It seems that every night after work, this amazingly dedicated athlete would scale the fence of the stadium where the track meet was held and work on his own for at least an hour before running the two miles to his home. It's the memories of stories such as this over the years that have made the long hours and short pay all worthwhile.

4. Psychological Problems

Regardless of the preconceived notions put forth by folks who have never donned a uniform, all athletes are not "dumb jocks." Also, as an obviously biased person, I have always believed that coaches are the best instructors in the teaching profession. Since I have been in the education field, the following "innovative practices" have been brought into the schools to improve the teaching and learning process: team teaching, idea sharing, a multitude of teacher-evaluation methods, inclusion, specialized instruction, teacher workshops and seminars—and the list could go on and on. The successful coach has been using every single one of these performance-enhancing initiatives for years, long before they were suggested and implemented by the rest of the educational community, and as I have already pointed out, the old coach displays his product to thousands of evaluators every Friday night. If a person would do a demographic survey of every football team in America, he would soon conclude that they represent the *most diverse* "classrooms" on campus. On the same team, I have had the valedictorian line up beside the very special student who requires individual instruction in every class he attends—and they both performed well. Let me once again emphasize that football is much more difficult to teach and to learn than it appears from the fifty-yard line with a Coke and a bag of popcorn in your hands. A very conservative coach, such as John Meadows, will have at least twenty-five or thirty offensive plays to teach to eleven different positions for each game. Each one of these plays will have to be called and executed in twenty-five seconds against an assortment of possible defenses. He will also have four or five different defenses of his own to teach, with a variety of different alignments off each one of them for at least twelve to fifteen different offensive sets that his opponent will use in every game. Opponents will line up in one offensive set, and before the snap of the ball, they will motion or move to an entirely different one and that "dumb jock" has to recognize this and adjust in a matter of seconds. You also need to keep in mind that all of this teaching is taking place while your student is being subjected to physical stress, fatigue, inclement weather, and the pressures exerted by his desire to win and the expectations of his teammates and coaches—not to mention the thousands of fanatical people who paid five dollars to watch him perform what he has learned.

As mentioned, I have coached many players with varied mental capacities and problems. I'll mention two. First, there's the player with an IQ so high that it won't even fit on the scale. He was an offensive lineman and a pretty good one. With a young man such as this, the coaching methods are very different from those used to explain blocking rules and techniques to the average high school athlete. With this high achiever, each step and each motion *always* had to be followed by a valid reason or explanation. His reasoning and deductive skills were never on vacation, and he was constantly on alert for the slightest slip-up by his coach and did not mind raising his hand and correcting the perceived error. I recall one particular occasion when I was "in his face" emphasizing a certain mistake he kept repeating—when up went the hand. I responded with a very stern one-word reply: "*What*?!" This future brain surgeon stepped back, stroked his chin, and in his most matter-of-fact voice, he asked a question that brought nothing but silence from this surprised coach: "Coach, did you ever consider this? If I *never* messed up—you wouldn't have a job."

Then there's the athlete who *does* have a legitimate learning problem in a structured classroom and needs special attention there, as well as on the field. I am reminded of one in particular who had a hard time focusing and was quick to utter the words *I can't* (for me as well as for the English teacher). As with many of the students who have a learning disability, he had a very low self-esteem and not much confidence in anything he tried. This young man played center for me, and I have always asked the player at this position to make the necessary line calls for the rest of the offensive line. His peers realized his limitations, and as is often the case with teenage boys, they were less than complimentary with their remarks and derogatory names. After the first few practices, which had produced much embarrassing taunting from his teammates, he came to me when I was alone in my office and started the conversation with his two favorite words: "I can't...." I stopped him abruptly and informed him, "Not only *can* you make those calls, you *will* make them—*every one* of them—in Saturday's scrimmage." This meeting occurred on a Wednesday, so I knew I had three sessions to convince this capable and valuable player that he *could* learn and then to educate him in recognizing defenses and making the proper calls. He came to my house for supper that night after practice and I proceeded to line up various defenses in front of him in the form of my dining-room chairs. We started with the simple recognition of odd or even and progressed to the defensive alignments of head-up, inside, or outside. When he had mastered the identification of each defense, we plugged in the plays and the calls, and by Saturday morning when we had one last walk-through, I could line up the chairs and then "jitterbug" them to another look—and he still didn't miss a call. That afternoon after a quick "down there and back," we huddled the offense, and I brought my star pupil to the front and made the announcement that *he* would be making all the line calls during the scrimmage. I don't know what was the defining feature of that moment—the ear-to-ear smile of my excited and confident student or the bewildered stare of his apprehensive teammates. Not a call was missed during our two-hour skirmish, and when I pointed this out during the "everybody up—hit a knee" talk, this reassured, very special team member received a standing round of applause from the entire team. This young man was indeed *very special*. I *will* have to admit a slight modification I had to make in order for this special fellow to continue to adjust the blocking scheme at the line of scrimmage. It seems that he was so intent on recognizing the defense and making the correct call that if we changed the snap count to anything but one, he would forget to snap the ball. Simple adjustment—we moved him to tackle. He played right tackle on a state championship team, making all-conference and continuing his football career in college. Now *he* is the one who teaches the plays and calls to his own bunch of high school linemen.

5. School Problems

On more than one occasion, I have heard it suggested by some uninformed member of the academic world that football, and athletics in general, should be abolished so that more time and money could be spent on the *more important* aspects of a student's life. I also have had more than one of my players *retire* from the game because of parents who felt that his grades would improve if he no longer had to devote his precious time to "nothing more than a game." All my life I have heard the analogy (and used it many times myself) that *life* is a game that we begin to learn how to play from infancy. In this game of life, we soon learn that there are many players and many instructors, that the rules sometimes change, and that we need all the help we can get if we "play" it well. The poet John Donne said it best in his poem "Meditations": *"No man is an island."* I can also say without reservation that I have never had one of these *retirees'* grades suddenly improve, but, unfortunately the opposite is frequently the case. The concerned parents usually discover that football wasn't the culprit causing the deflated GPA but some other unrelated factor—not always but many times wearing a short skirt.

Of course, there are several other factors that may contribute to an athlete's academic problems. Included in these, and usually not far down the list, is a student's previous educational background. When the program you establish is successful, it won't be a secret. That recruiting process I mentioned earlier, which not only is unethical but also illegal, will not be necessary if the reason for your success is established through those factors that I have previously outlined. Your colleagues, boosters, and the general members of your community will become salesmen for your program throughout the area. Parents concerned not only with the athletic accomplishments of their child but also with their scholastic achievements (or lack of) have, *of their own choice*, made a bona fide move to associate their youngster with our program. Invariably, those involved on the other side of the move will declare "foul" and accuse you of illegal recruiting and usually have the state athletic department conduct an investigation. Throughout the many decades I have spent on the sidelines, I have had this accusation made a few times. I can honestly say that I have never been guilty of that illegal form of recruitment, but the consistency of winning seasons and a legitimate concern for the *total* success of my players have placed some pretty decent football players in my huddle on Friday night. I have explained all of that to introduce a couple of stories about how we helped to solve academic problems that surfaced because of a lack of genuine involvement in that aspect of these young men's lives.

My first example involves a player who showed up before pre-season practice one day and explained that he had just moved into our neighborhood and would like to play ball for us. He proceeded to relate to the coaches his story about a family conflict—involving an abusive father, among other problems—which necessitated his moving to our school district. This very pleasant, polite, and respectful fellow was moving from a smaller school where in most classes "Yes, Ma'am" and "No, Ma'am" would get you at least a C. Although we do insist that our players be the most respectful students in class, we also expect them to do enough work to *earn* that C. Evidently, there was at least one person in his last school who had those same expectations: his English teacher. His eligibility depended on his passing an English class in summer school. Like the young man already mentioned, he too had to maintain a job that summer to assist with the financial element of his family. His work schedule would not allow him to attend the regular summer school, so we improvised. I have a minor in English, and through special arrangements made with the principal, I became his summer school English teacher and the football field house, his classroom. I must mention that this future NFL player was also very involved with his church; consequently, the Bible became his English textbook for that summer school session. Each day after he got off work, he would make his way to the field house, climb on top of the equipment cage, and open his "Holy textbook." We used one of the new translations that uses modern English words, and I would have him read certain passages to me from atop the wire mesh cage. I would stop him, ask questions, and make comments as we worked on his vocabulary and comprehension. We covered nouns, pronouns, verbs, adjectives, prepositions, and all the rest of the parts of speech that Paul, Peter, James, and the rest of the inspired writers used to convey to us the Word of God. I understand that today there are missionaries who go into foreign countries and teach English through the Bible. This may be a somewhat new technique to those using it, but "Old John" came up with it forty years ago. Although his responses to me were still the respectful "Yes, Sir" and "No, Sir," that is not what *earned* him his C but rather his dedicated effort and hard work. Did this special class and the high expectations of his regular teachers help him? There is a letter of commendation from the college he attended where he made not only the athletic all-conference team but, more impressive, was also selected *academic* all-conference.

This next story that involves solving problems in school is not about an individual but an entire team. Many years before state athletic departments decided that all athletes need a C average before they can participate in their respective sports, I had already determined that grades should be high up the priority list of the guys who performed for me on Friday night. As you read this, keep in mind that we're talking about many years ago when *everyone* realized the importance of discipline—not only at home but also at school—and particularly in athletics. The *"board of education"* was usually made of hickory and was about two feet long. (In this era, "time out" was a rest period you got three of during each half of a football game. If you got a paddling at school, one thing was for sure—you got another one at home by supportive parents. Times have changed, and when I read the headlines of the paper every morning, in my opinion, this change has not been for the better.) As I have mentioned, I have always made it a practice to emphasize the importance of my players' performance both on and off the field—and especially academically in the classroom. All of my life I've heard the expression, "Forewarned is fore learned." Obviously, the players on this particular team had not. During one of the first meetings with our team at this new school, I *emphatically* warned them that anything less than a C on their first report card would not be acceptable and also made it clear what the consequences would be otherwise. I also reminded them of this at each "Everybody up" at the end of practice. Six weeks passed and the day of reckoning arrived. At the beginning of sixth period, we had a manager stand in the door of the field house and instruct the players as they came in not to get dressed but to line up in front with report cards in hand. We need to go to "Mr. Webster" to describe exactly what was about to take place just prior to practice on this cool October afternoon. <u>*Motivate*</u>—*"To stimulate to action; provide with an incentive or motive; impel; incite."* At this time I had four varsity coaches who also formed a line in front of the field house, each equipped with a hickory "motivational device" about two feet long. (There are two groups of people who may not need to read the rest of this section of dialogue: squeamish mamas who can't stand the thoughts of inflicting pain on their little darlings and liberal "baby boomers" who might want to check the statute of limitations on child abuse.) As the team started through the gauntlet, I checked the cards and passed on the information to the other four coaches: "Two D's and an F." That would equal three *"stimulating"* swings of the *"board of education"* by each of the four coaches. Did this archaic form of discipline perform its desired effect and *provide the incentive* that this particular collection of uninspired athletes needed? We didn't have to wait another six weeks to find out. Almost every teacher on the staff declared that she had never seen a group of students have such an attitude change. The next six weeks' line was considerably shorter.

PART III

CHARACTER TRAITS OF THE COACH WHO IS A TRUE LEADER

Chapter 3

Qualities for the Coach To Develop for Success

Integrity

Discerning what is right and wrong, acting on what you have discerned (even at personal cost), and admitting openly that *your actions are based* on your understanding of right and wrong—this is who you *really* are. People may forget your won-lost record or that state championship you won back whenever, but they will always remember if you were an honest man whose word was his bond. This is especially true of the young people whose minds you help to mold and whose characters are based on what they see exemplified in those they respect the most.

Friendship

Will Rogers once said, "I never met a man I didn't like." (All I can say is that he never met some of the irate parents I have observed during my fifty-plus years of coaching and teaching.) I mention this to magnify the need for good friends at your workplace. It is these friends who make it easier to come to work every day. I've already talked about the importance of befriending your colleagues in the teaching and coaching profession, but this is just as true concerning *all* of those with whom you must work every day. *Good friends* are still your *friends* on Monday morning when time ran out on you on Friday night.

Courage

The *ability* to make any decision has to be accompanied by the *courage* to do so. Every coach has to make unpopular decisions. You *are* going to be second-guessed and criticized. It comes with the job. You don't have at your disposal popularity polls when it's fourth and two on the goal line. What you *do* have is twenty-five seconds to make a decision, and whether you hear boos or cheers following that decision depends on the training and execution of eleven teenage boys.

Exemplary Work Ethic

This quality *is* contagious. Both the players and the other coaches will catch this attribute if they are exposed to it enough. Long hours in coaching are necessary, but they must also be meaningful. I learned a long time ago that after two hours—you're coaching yourself! Coaches don't punch a clock, so when the job is finished, don't stay and keep the other coaches and team involved in solidifying *your* reputation as a hard worker—"Go home to Mama!"

Perseverance

I've never met anyone in the coaching profession who *likes* to lose. On the other hand, I've never met anyone who hasn't lost. There are two important things that the coaches—and the team—must always consider: "You can't continue to *celebrate* your victories, and you can't continue to *wallow* in your defeats!"

Loyalty

I've touched on this very important aspect of coaching before, but I emphasize again that my job should always be to make the person above me look better. We *all* are responsible to *someone*. Whether we like them or dislike them has nothing to do with our responsibility to be loyal. This does *not* mean that we must agree with them on everything. Loyalty is a two-way street. Not only do I expect those guys who coach for me to *be loyal to me and to the program*, but also I am duty-bound to *be loyal to them* and to solicit their input regarding any decision that affects them and the team. Any successful person in a leadership role, including head coaches, encourages the well-thought-out and productive ideas of others. This being true, it is also understood that the *final* decision goes to the one who must accept the responsibility if it is a bad one.

Thoroughness

Whose mother hasn't said, "If it is worth doing at all, do it right"? I've told every team that I've ever coached that they all should strive to be the best they can be in whatever they are doing. If you're a ditch digger, be the *best* ditch digger around. DO SOMETHING! Take action. Make a decision. You must be so thorough in your preparation that you know enough about the situation to make that decision a *wise* one. (For the old coach, it's like 4th and a foot on the twenty-yard line going in.)

Humility

I will later explain in detail the importance of this leadership quality in the young man whom you choose as your quarterback. You, as a coach, to be the type of leader necessary to be successful, must also exhibit this same humility. This is pretty easy when you suffer a defeat, but it takes some work if you amass a string of victories. It's then that it's hard to remember one of the basic laws of science: "What goes up must come down!" We are also reminded of this in the words of Christ in Luke 14:11: *"For everyone that exalts himself shall be humbled, and he who humbles himself shall be exalted."* The following story exemplifies the need for this characteristic very well: A young "rookie" preacher came into the pulpit at his new congregation for his first sermon. He was very self-confident and smug—really cocky! He was very well-dressed with not a hair out of place; he *knew* he had what it took. He strutted into the pulpit and began to deliver his first sermon, but when he started to speak, the words simply wouldn't come out. He choked. Humiliated, he burst into tears and ended up leaving the platform, obviously humbled. There were two little old ladies sitting on the first row, and one turned to the other and said, "If he had come *in* like he went out, he would have gone *out* like he came in!"

Wisdom

I didn't say *knowledge*! Dispensing knowledge is the job of your teachers and coaches. There's nothing wrong with knowledge—we must have it. To be the effective leader *you* want to be, you *must* acquire *wisdom*. I believe that the longevity and success of any coach depend on this quality more than any other. For that reason I will dwell on it more than the other qualities because they are *all* attained through *this* attribute. Take a look at Proverbs 4:5–9 and listen to the advice of King David, the father of the wisest man who has ever lived: *⁵Get wisdom! Get understanding! Do not forget, nor turn away from the words of my mouth. ⁶Do not forsake her, and she will preserve you; Love her, and she will keep you. ⁷Wisdom is the principal thing; Therefore get wisdom. And in all your getting, get understanding. ⁸Exalt her, and she will promote you; She will bring you honor, when you embrace her. ⁹She will place on your head an ornament of grace; A crown of glory she will deliver to you.*

Wisdom in our lives is gained through one of two sources—years of trial and error or the proven experience of others. If the wisdom we have accumulated is primarily a product of the first option, we can rest assured that any success we may have enjoyed could have been greatly enhanced and accelerated had we employed the second. Many times, an idea may *look good* on paper, but when we try to *implement* it, we can't believe we even *tried* it. Especially in our profession, the old proverb "If at first you don't succeed, try, try again" has been tested, and its necessary relevance has been proven over and over again. So often the "try, try again" part is due to our own stubborn will. As the title of this book indicates, winning is not totally dependent on X's and O's but is often brought about through the application of the proven coaching philosophies and techniques of others in the same line of work. When we think of the time we've wasted on countless unsuccessful *trials,* we also must consider the unforeseen consequences of the *errors* of many wrong decisions. It's true that we *can* gain wisdom this way—*if* we survive those errors. The problem is that our survival (our job) usually depends on the ratio of success and error depicted in the won-lost column of our resume.

A few years ago, there was an article in the *American Football Monthly* about Mickey Andrews, the defensive coordinator at Florida State University. Upon receiving the Broyles Award, given to the top assistant in the nation, Andrews quickly switched the attention to the runner-up, Nebraska's Charlie McBride, as he stated, "A lot of what we do defensively we got from other people—like Charlie—it's not something we came up with ourselves." McBride agreed but said, "What makes Andrews different is that he'll admit it. A lot of coaches won't!"

Part IV

Divine Wisdom

CHAPTER 4

Divine Wisdom: Defined by James 3:16–17 and Applied to the Coaching Profession

Biblical Principles of Wisdom

Before we leave this topic of wisdom, I want to go back to my source book for a description of *divine wisdom* given to us by James that has practical application to the coach who desires to be a good, effective leader.

James Chapter 3:16–17

16 For where jealousy and selfish ambition exist, there is disorder and every evil thing.
17 But the wisdom from above is first <u>pure</u>, then <u>peaceable</u>, <u>gentle</u>, <u>reasonable</u>, <u>full of mercy</u> and <u>good fruits</u>, <u>unwavering</u>, <u>without hypocrisy</u>.

<u>Pure</u>—Good morals help to gain respect from even the "baddest of apples." Insist that players and coaches alike do *nothing* to embarrass the team.

<u>Peaceable</u>—This helps us establish rapport—the right relationship with those *for* whom you work and *with* whom you work: administrators/teachers/students/parents.

<u>Gentle</u>—This quality means to be patient under provocation. Be fair and treat others as you want to be treated.

<u>Reasonable</u>—You must prove yourself approachable—not so stubborn that you can't be convinced that you're wrong—when you really are. Don't project yourself as *perfect* and therefore be so rigid that you won't listen and consider the ideas and advice of others.

<u>Full of Mercy</u>—Compassionate—Young coaches (old ones too) should be reminded again and again that "If they ain't out there, we can't help them!" I can't over-emphasize the importance of discipline in all aspects of life, and it certainly holds true when dealing with your football team. Unfortunately, there comes a time and a set of circumstances, after you have exhausted all means to reclaim the wayward athlete, when you have to "fire" one for the betterment of the team. This was always the hardest part of my job as the head coach. I was always reminded of the story of John Bradford, a clergyman of the 1500s. While performing his duties as a chaplain at a prison in

England, each time he watched the condemned prisoners going to their execution, he is said to have remarked, "There but for the grace of God go *I*."

Full of Good Fruits—Produce! The *fruit expected* from the coach is W's on Friday night. This *will* happen if he has the proper seed (adequate personnel), prepares the soil (trains them well), and nourishes the plant (practice, practice, practice). There's not a coach anywhere who likes to win more than John Meadows. Producing those wins certainly was enjoyable and satisfying, but the *real fruit* created by *any* coach worth his salt is much more tangible. Naturally, my goal each season was to win every game on our schedule, but beyond that I wanted every player I coached to become someone's *best neighbor*.

Unwavering—Consistent—Keep an open mind and be willing to be unpopular to be right. Dealing with people can become very difficult if you don't treat them all the same. We all know that it's easy to discipline "a thug." To gain and maintain the respect needed to be successful, we must handle *him* the same as we do the star player who is also president of the student body. Even *bad* referees are tolerated if they are *consistent*.

Without Hypocrisy—Be honest. Be *real*. Kids can spot a hypocrite more quickly than anyone else, and like all of us, they can't stand them! This is much like a *Ford* salesman driving his *Chevy* home each night after work. (Jesus used this derogatory term describing His adversaries seventeen times in the book of Matthew.)

The best coaches are those who surround themselves with leaders and delegate authority. They let them coach! The worst try to coach it all themselves.

An ancient Chinese philosopher once said:

> "As for the best leaders, the people do not notice their existence. The next best, the people honor and praise. The next, the people fear, and the next, the people hate. When the best leader's work is done, the people say, 'We did it ourselves.'"

Conclusion

There may be some highly successful folks in the business or professional world who would look at the teaching and coaching profession and shake their heads and say, "What a bunch of losers!" That may be so if your scoreboard has dollar signs on it, but if represented there are the lives of real people and you're graded on the difference you made in those lives. **BALL GAME! WE WIN!**

PART V

ATTITUDES TO BE DEVELOPED IN THE WINNING ATHLETE

CHAPTER 5

Intrinsic Values To Instill and To Expand in Our Athletes

Academics

Life doesn't end at the goal line. Not too many job interviews begin with "What's your best 40 time?" or "What was the score of your last ball game?" Colleges and employers are more interested in your ACT score and your GPA than they are your best max on the bench or your yards per carry. I tried to end each practice with a "Gather up, hit a knee" pep talk. In this talk, after the usual football stuff, I always mentioned what we expected of our players in the classroom. I wanted them to leave the field every day realizing that there *is* an afterlife following their football career and that their success in that endeavor depended on what they did in the first six hours of the school day—not just the last three.

Dedication

I'll do whatever it takes! Losing is easy—all you have to do is *nothing*. In 1965 Benny Marshall, who was the sports editor for *The Birmingham News* at the time, wrote a book entitled *WINNING ISN'T EVERYTHING *But it beats anything that comes in second.* This book outlined the life and attitude of one of the greatest coaches of all time—Paul "Bear" Bryant. In the book Marshall quotes an ex-Tide player's telling why Alabama won under the direction of Coach Bryant. "The reason Alabama wins is because everybody gives all they've got. That's what Coach Bryant wants, and that's what he gets." To be dedicated is to be committed—to *something*. Our job as coaches is to direct that commitment toward the positive rather than the negative.

Team-Player Attitude

"*We,*" not "*me.*" There is an old saying that I have heard basketball coaches declare to their teams over and over again: "You'll score more points if you don't care who shoots." This particular attitude is pretty easy to instill into the offensive linemen who, for the most part, are being watched during the game by only their mamas. It's mostly the guys that score the touchdowns or have their names called out several times over the loudspeakers for tackles made that need to be reminded of this important aspect of a winning team. Not very often, but once or twice through the years, I have had that self-centered running back that got a bad case of "me-itis," and as my daddy used to say, "Got a little too big for his breeches." I had the perfect way to turn his conceit into gratitude. I'd announce that we were going to have a goal-line scrimmage, and after the defense lined up, I'd tell the quarterback and "Mr. Touchdown" to get in the backfield and run Power Right on one. "Where's the line?" was the look on his face—as well as the words in his mouth. This lesson in Appreciation 101 usually *did not* have to be repeated.

Drive and Determination

If you ever meet the coach who can guarantee you he can instill these two factors in every player, try to hire him, but definitely *don't* put him on your schedule! It's these two dynamics that are behind most all of the great success stories in America. It was drive and determination that put men on the moon. It was drive and determination that put a Wal-Mart store in almost every town you drive through. In the realm of athletics, the list of heroes who owe their achievements to these components would swamp this page. Lou Gehrig, Stan Musial, Ted Williams, Cal Ripkin, Jesse Owens, Johnny Unitas, Gayle Sayers, and Wilma Rudolph represent only the tip of the iceberg of those great athletes who can head the inventory of contributing factors for their successes with these two words: *drive* and *determination.*

I've made many mistakes during my half-century in this sport, too many to report. One characteristic that I possessed as a young coach that led to many of those mistakes was *impatience*. I found myself wanting to get everything done—right now! Many young coaches (including me) have let this negative characteristic run off at least one or two potentially "good 'uns." Not all of the young men who came to me were blessed with the physical stature or the mental resolve to have immediate success in athletics. Many were a *"mama's boy"* whose *daddy* wanted his son to give him something to brag about every Monday morning by the water fountain at work. We all know that there is not a machine or a magic potion that can be used for such a transformation. As high school coaches, each of us can compose our own list of players who overcame seemingly insurmountable obstacles to play and often excel in this game of football and even in life itself. Size, strength, speed, lack of desire, home life, and many times a combination of some or all of these barriers were overcome by many young men just to compete in this man's game called football. I could tell many inspirational and very touching accounts concerning young men who had to rise above difficult situations that often render lesser men to obscurity. I'll mention two of these fellows who, although several years apart, had an almost identical set of circumstances as well as eventual outcomes. Both of these young gentlemen were offensive linemen and had the same physical build—so much so that they both were labeled with the same nickname by their teammates: "Dough Boy."

This *was* an appropriate title for the first three years of their participation since their resemblance to the Pillsbury icon *was* unmistakable. They were clumsy, weak, and slow, but dedicated to the task before them. Each of these fellows continued to work hard and to grow both in strength and in size. The metamorphosis was slow but steady, and it was gratifying as a coach to watch these inept "little boys" developing into respected young men and really good football players. Both were starters as seniors, and both earned all-city and all-region honors. One was awarded a scholarship to an SEC school, where he was selected as an all-conference guard his final year. The other, who wasn't quite as tall, received a scholarship to an OVC powerhouse, where he too was an all-conference performer.

Leadership (Servant)

Mark 9:35: *"And He sat down, and called the twelve, and saith unto them, If any man desire to be first, the same shall be last of all, and servant of all."*

This Biblical reference to humility should be an abiding principle in every phase of our lives and definitely has application on the athletic field. I will cover more extensively this vital component of leadership in the winning athlete when discussing the quarterback position. It is an accepted given that the guy who directs your offense *must* have this important characteristic if your team is going to have any success, but I constantly preach this to the *entire* team. The more leaders that you have, the easier your job is—and the more games you will win. During one of the worst seasons that I can recall over the past half-century that *leader* never did surface despite the coaches' constant asking for one to step forward. We were in the dressing room at halftime during a very hard-fought contest with our biggest rival, and the "asking" for leadership had reached the "begging and pleading" stage when one of the players stood up. This was a good kid, a decent athlete—but certainly *not* a leader. As he stood up on the bench, he shouted, "Listen to me!" He then proceeded to shout several times at the top of his lungs, "I am your leader!" The response he received from the rest of the team, who knew him well, was not the crescendo of confident "Let's go get 'ums" but very blank stares followed by deafening silence. We took the field the second half just as we had in the first—without a leader—and we left the field with one of our losses. I've always told my players, "If you're good, you won't have to hang a sign around your neck saying it—people will figure it out on their own!" *True* leaders *never* have to make that declaration, and if they do, they usually are *not*.

Competitiveness

In every game I ever coached, I wanted to win, I liked to win, I *expected* to win. Losing was *not* an acceptable option. The players I coached knew this, and the vast majority of them felt the same way I did. Winning becomes a habit. Unfortunately, so does losing. When *we* lost a game, it was usually as much a surprise as it was a disappointment. The word *championship* was always included somewhere in our written and *expected* goals every year. When I think of a competitor, I can still see in my mind's eye that hard-nosed linebacker hobbling onto the field for the championship game with a knee so swollen that each step was more painful than the last. I still see the tears rolling down the face of the defensive tackle after playing the game of his life three days after burying his devoted father. I see the pride of accomplishment in the faces of scores of young men—those who were told all their lives that they were too small, too slow, or not good enough—as they walked off the field with headgears held high in a victory salute after contributing to a big win for the team. It's the challenge of competition and the desire to excel, despite all odds, that separate the *winner* from the *also-ran* on the football field—*and* afterwards.

Confidence

Confidence is a direct product of preparation. That mid-term algebra test isn't nearly as intimidating to the student who has applied himself all semester and stayed up all night studying. There is a fine line between confidence and cockiness, although the first should produce a certain degree of the second. I always wanted the team that I was coaching to take the field with a little swagger in their steps, enough to show that other bunch that we *were ready to play*. I remember that growing up back in Cedar Creek, the dog that usually won the fight was the one that strutted around with bristles on his back scratching the dirt, not the one with his tail tucked between his legs. An important coaching point: place one word in front of this trait, and it usually spells disaster. That word is *over*. This usually occurs when you have won four or five big games and your next opponent is "0'fer." This is especially true when those losses have been close games with respectable teams. In this situation teenage kids and young coaches (and sometimes old ones) are very susceptible to that "over" word—and certain defeat. I'll admit that I have been guilty of *over*confidence once or twice over the past fifty years when I failed to prepare my team properly, both physically *and* mentally, and we had to ride back home on a silent bus—with that tail tucked between *my* legs.

Discipline

I've already discussed my thoughts on having a list of rules posted on the wall. I have found that discipline derived from a checklist of do's and don'ts is very superficial and can be, in certain situations, counterproductive to your coaching obligations. The discipline needed to win ball games comes through long hours of hard work—training the mind and body to perform acceptably under all conditions. This type of discipline is what your team needs in the final minutes of the fourth quarter when the winning touchdown is ten yards away. When your mind and body are exhausted, performance is drawn from the instruction that is realized during those grueling hours on the practice field and the discipline gained by them.

Realism

By this I mean: when it's over, it's over. We must relish our victories and learn from our defeats, but we can't dwell on either one. Very often, this quality is as difficult to acquire for the coach as it is for the players. Many times, the most difficult job we have as coaches is dealing with the player who dropped the winning touchdown pass or fumbled the ball on the one-yard line while going in for the winning touchdown. We can't afford to allow one mistake to destroy that special attribute we discussed—confidence—so important to the winning program. I recall a particular time when my best receiver dropped the go-ahead touchdown in the end zone and came to the sidelines with that "hang-dog" look on his face. Realizing the importance of attitude, regardless of the skill level, I grabbed him by his facemask and pulled him to the side, and by the look in his eyes, I perceived that he thought he was going to get a good butt-chewing. I placed both hands on his shoulder pads, looked him in the eyes, and in a very calm voice, I told him, "Listen to me, son. Whether we win or lose this game tonight, the sun will still come up tomorrow, and you'll *still* be my best receiver. Forget that one and catch the next one." I added with a grin, "I think I dropped one back in 1945." That last statement brought a smile to his face and the twinkle back in his eyes. He *did* catch the next one—and the next one—and one more on the tips of his fingers as he dragged his feet in the corner of the end zone. Ball game!

Toughness—Physical and Mental

Football is a contact sport! When young men cover their bodies with twenty pounds of equipment and run into each other while moving at full speed, there is going to be a certain degree of pain involved. When we speak of a player's being "physically tough," we mean that he knows the difference between being *hurt* and being *injured*. I have never *asked*, nor *expected*, anyone to perform when he was *injured*, but I *have* had many to "suck up" a jammed thumb or a bruised muscle. I don't recall being in many dressing rooms that did not display a placard somewhere on the wall that declared "WHEN THE GOING GETS TOUGH, THE TOUGH GET GOING." There are many lifelong lessons to be learned in the game of football, but one would be very hard-pressed to name one that is more important in the game of life than this one. The older I get, the more "hurts" I wake up with every morning, but still vivid in my mind is a portion of "The Ballad of Sir Andrew" I had hanging in my dressing room that inspired *me* more than once to press on: *"Fight on my men," Sir Andrew said, "A little I'm hurt, but not yet slain; I'll just lie down and bleed awhile, then rise and fight again."*

Mental toughness is difficult to separate from the physical, and in the game of football and, indeed, in life itself, they each play an equal role in producing qualities that enhance our success in either. I am reminded of a version of an inspirational poem by Walter D. Wintle that I had attached to that same bulletin board. Its following message encourages our development of that confidence needed to perform to our greatest potential:

It's All in a State of Mind

If you think you are beaten, you are;
If you think you dare not, you won't.
If you like to win but don't think you can,
It's almost a cinch you won't.

If you think you'll lose, you're lost,
For out in the world you'll find
Success begins with a fellow's will—
It's all in a state of mind.

For many a game is lost
Ere even a play is run,
And many a coward fails
Ere even his work is begun.

Think big, and your deeds will grow.
Think small, and you'll fall behind.

Think that you CAN and you WILL—
It's all in a state of mind.

If you think you are out-classed, you are.
You've got to think high to rise.
You've got to be sure of yourself before
You can ever win a prize.

Life's battles don't always go
To the stronger or faster man,
But sooner or later the man who wins
Is the fellow who THINKS he can.

If you *think* you're tough, you probably are! Basically, it means that you are able to take constructive criticism in a tone somewhat above a whisper. Really, constructive criticism is what *all* coaching boils down to after a certain point. Why would I sometimes raise my voice on the football field? It's for the same reasons I would *not* say in a *mild* manner, "Don't touch that handle—it's hot"—importance and urgency. There are many players that we have to "coach out" of what I call the "only child syndrome." When there are several siblings running around the house, they all get used to hearing "No" more times than "OK," and usually that *is* above a whisper. We're back now to that parent conference when we convinced Mama and Daddy that our coaching techniques are designed to do more than win ball games.

Part VI

Tips for Victory

CHAPTER 6

Guidelines I've Used Through the Years

Match Up Players

Don't *waste* one of your good players on their best stud, offensive or defensive. If the other bunch has an all-state offensive lineman and we don't have the corresponding counterpart, we put a "frog" on him and cut him. The same is true with our best receiver. We want our best to go against their worst. We will avoid their best defensive back even if we have to motion to do it. There have been times when I have been blessed with studs of my own, and we have installed in our game-plan plays designed to show off our guys and to discourage theirs. Two examples of this are worth the telling.

The first involves an out-of-state team who had a nose man in their fifty defense with the nickname "The Wild Bunch" after the outlaw gang made famous by the popular movie of the time *Butch Cassidy and the Sundance Kid*. We had films of this fellow destroying offensive linemen with his quickness and aggressiveness. That year, our offensive line wasn't all that bad either—four of them signed college scholarships. I have described the lead play that was one of the staples of our offense where we double-teamed the nose and blocked the linebacker with the fullback. Our offensive-line coach had a term he used with his linemen: "ten dollar block." He told them if they blocked their man ten yards down the field that he would give them a ten-dollar bill. (With him grading the film, the good blocks were usually declared to be nine-and-one-half yards—"close, but no cigar.") No surprise. We ran that lead play about twenty times that night, and on several of those plays, "The Wild Bunch" looked as if he had on roller skates instead of cleats. We never tried to hurt anyone badly intentionally, but with about four minutes gone in the third quarter, "The Wild Bunch" (after his nine-and-a-half-yard ride) was taken to the sidelines on a cart and never returned to the game.

This next story is much like the first. It, too, involves an out-of-state team that we picked up just before the season started. A little over a week before our first ball game, I received a phone call from the executive secretary of the Alabama High School Athletic Association. He said that he had a call from a wealthy football booster in this out-of-state town who had a son who played for the local team. This fellow was an avid University of Alabama fan and a devoted follower of their legendary coach Bear Bryant. His son, a defensive lineman, had always wanted to play for the Bear, but the state where he played was not known for their football, and he was afraid that his son would go unnoticed by this major university. His solution was to call the AHSAA and see if a highly respected team in Alabama might have the same open date as his son's school. His plan was to send the tape of the game to Coach

Bryant and let him witness how well his son did against an Alabama powerhouse. Back in this time before area and region play, the more games you won, the harder it was to schedule games. We did have the same open date, and I was glad to give this gentleman a call and see if we could do business. After talking to this booster-turned-schedule-maker, I decided very quickly that "wealthy" was an inadequate expression to describe his worth. This was to be over a 200-mile trip and would entail a meal on the way, feeding the team after the game, and spending the night. When this fellow explained what he had in mind, I knew that it was a deal I shouldn't refuse. He first asked me about our band. I proudly told him that we had a band of over one hundred members that was well known all over the South as one of the best. "Will they come if I pay their expenses?" I assured him that they would be delighted. He told me that he would pay all of our expenses, including motel rooms for our team and our band plus a meal after the game for both and a very generous monetary guarantee. Of course I accepted, trying not to seem *too* overly eager. As luck would have it, the week before we played this team, they had a Saturday night game about 150 miles from our school that all our coaches were able to scout. We arrived at the stadium about an hour before the game, and as we walked around the track, headed for the bleachers, an unfamiliar voice called out, "Coach." We all turned in response and saw a heavy-set, middle-aged man leaning over the fence, motioning for us to come his way. The red Alabama sweatshirt he was wearing in this rival state gave me a pretty good clue to who he was. "Coach Meadows?" he asked, as he pointed his finger back and forth between the seven coaches standing and staring at this stranger who seemed to recognize us three hours from home. Of course, we all had on coaching shirts with our school logo, which was a pretty good clue to who we were. After I stepped forward and identified myself, he invited us to the press box for some refreshments—provided by him (of course). Even though this game was almost a hundred miles from our opponent's school, this fellow seemed to be very much in charge as he introduced us to the other coaches in the press box, those from both schools. During the course of the contest, the coaches in the press box called down to the ones on the sidelines several times and held up their iced drinks and hotdogs and taunted them with, "Eat your heart out." All our coaches agreed that the atmosphere of the game was somewhat less intense than that which we were accustomed to back in Alabama. Each of our coaches had a particular assignment on each offensive and defensive play during the game, and we came home with a pretty decent scouting report. I focused most of my attention on the rich guy's son, expecting to see some animal wreaking havoc on the opposing team's offensive line. He *looked* good—standing six feet four inches and weighing in at about 270 pounds—but he *played* badly. Throughout my coaching career, it has been my observation that through their father's eyes there have been several "*all-state*" candidates who didn't receive that vote from a more impartial and knowledgeable panel. This seemed to be the case here, and I really hated to be the pin that would burst his balloon the next Friday night.

We didn't show a film on this team, fearing that it would cause our team's confidence level to soar to the point of possible defeat. Instead, we used the old ploy of "They wouldn't even give us a film" to help "fire up" our guys. We left early Friday morning, timing our arrival at a country food buffet on the way (known by our bus driver) right at lunchtime. Upon our arrival at the school in the mid-afternoon, it was not a surprise to see a fine-looking field house with a sign bearing the name of our benefactor hanging over the entrance. We unloaded our gear and were then escorted to a very nice motel where this "stud's" daddy had reserved most of the facility for us. We traveled with sixty-six players, eight coaches, our managers and trainer, and the bus driver and his son, so we had forty rooms. There weren't but two to a room, so each of the players had his own bed in which to relax for a couple of hours.

We arrived at the stadium about an hour and a half before kickoff, walked around the field to stretch our legs, and got the first look at our opponent. Their players were lying around the front of their dressing room in game pants and shimmy shirts, "eyeballing" this bunch of rednecks from Alabama. Our kids were observably impressed with what they saw—a bunch of good-sized, square-jawed athletes with no-nonsense expressions on their rugged faces as we strolled by them.

Kickoff was at 7:30, and despite the distance, we took the field to the encouraging cheers of four chartered busloads of our loyal supporters. There was a capacity crowd that (I'm sure) expected to see their local heroes send this bunch back to Alabama with firsthand knowledge of just how the game of football *should* be played. I've always been up for a challenge, and when someone makes three or four long-distance phone calls and spends enough money to pay off my house just to get to play me—I consider *that* a challenge! A very popular song of this time by Jim Croce probably depicts my attitude better than anything I could come up with—and it goes like this:

> *You don't tug on Superman's cape*
> *You don't spit into the wind*
> *You don't pull the mask off that old Lone Ranger*
> *And you don't mess around with Jim!*

The same can be said of "old John"! This team's defense was somewhat different from the fifty-look popular back home in Alabama. They played a 4–4 with the highlighted stud playing the strong-side 3 technique. As you will see later, we *are* going to run the football, and we *are* going to run off-tackle. We modified our blocking just a tad to check this perceived stud's oil. I figured that if he had a good game against what we were going to throw at him, the "Bear" himself would fly up and sign him. Our plan was to run right at him. We double-teamed him, kicked out with the fullback, and led through with the setback out of our Power I set. On numerous plays our two linemen assigned to perform this double team would "flat-back" our potential "Crimson Tider" just inches short of that ten-dollar bill. It was obvious that the play announcer understood his role and who it was who paid most of the bills. On almost every play this young man's name was announced as being "on the tackle." The truth was that he *was near* the pile but usually *under* it on his back some ten yards or so down the field. By halftime the only ones in the stands who were cheering were our band and four busloads of spectators. The score was Visitors 28—Disappointed Home Team 0. We had one touchdown and three long runs called back—which is always expected when you play this far away from home. In the second half, I showed what a nice fellow I am as we scored only one more touchdown—just to prove that we could—then I put the "big dogs" in the back of the truck and played everybody who had made the trip.

After the game it was a very shocked and frustrated daddy who came on the field with the coaches to shake our hands and to congratulate what he declared to be "the best team that has ever played on this field." I will never forget that game and the hospitality that was shown to everyone who made the trip. I don't know whatever happened to our aspiring athlete, but I do know this: a certain gruff-talking coach back in Alabama never got to take a look at him.

As Much As Possible, Have Somebody on the Center

I want one of my best defensive players to play against a "one-armed man." Quickness is the key ingredient I would look for in this "play disrupter" lined up in front of what usually is one of their best blockers. We've all known since we first strapped on a jock that games are won or lost by inches and fraction of seconds. I call the center a "one-armed man" that he is for that fraction of a second when his snapping hand is delivering the ball to his quarterback. We drill the nose man year-round to react to the first quiver of the football, and we expect to have at least one bad exchange fumble in every game. If I'm lucky enough to have a nose man who possesses size along with that quickness, I will employ the read technique with him along with the slant and blast technique. By the time the last horn blows, we will have produced a very frustrated center who will not grade very high during the Saturday morning evaluation.

Scout Yourself

Don't be predictable. Remember that you are not the only guy around who has the word *COACH* stenciled on his shirts. Each week, as I view my game film, I ask myself, "What would I do to beat 'Old John?'" If the film shows that the previous team had success against us with a certain play or offensive set, I would analyze the situation closely and try to determine the reason. It may be as simple as "Their guys whipped our guys," and if so, there's not a whole lot that can be done about that in a week. What you *can* do something about is poor alignment or improper adjustment. By the next week's game, these things *can* be ironed out if they are noticed and addressed. In games that I feel I can win, I try to have two or three special sets and plays and even defensive alignments that I know I wouldn't use in a big game. The next coach I'm playing doesn't know that, and I'm assured that he will waste valuable practice time preparing for them. I have always enjoyed playing with the mind of the other team's coach, especially those that I know well. One year we were playing a cross-town rival in a very important contest. We both had exceptional teams and had a lot riding on the outcome of this particular game. On Sunday afternoon I sent two of my assistants to their school to swap films. Before they left our field house, we diagrammed a "special" game plan using some pretty exotic sets and defensive alignments that our coaches planned to "lose" at their place. They found all of their coaches in a meeting room, sitting around waiting for our film. After a few minutes of lies and buttering up each other, one of our coaches nonchalantly reached into his back pocket for a handkerchief to stifle a make-believe cough and in the process pulled out the "game plan" that fell to the floor. They said that every coach's eye followed it down and then quickly snapped back as if nothing had happened. Needless to say, *our* preparation that week did not involve those special sets and defenses, but according to their coaches' affirmation after the game (that *we* won), *theirs* did.

Teach Your Linemen Every Offensive-Line Position

We want to have the best players in the game. We don't want to have a guard injured and a second-team *tackle* that is better than the second-team *guard* standing on the sidelines. There's only one specialist on the offensive line—the center. Not every lineman will be capable of bringing the ball up to the quarterback while simultaneously executing a block on who is usually the toughest defensive lineman on the opposing team, but during off-season drills, we always prepare as many players as possible to perform this maneuver. Some years when I'm blessed with several capable offensive linemen, I have given instructions to certain selected players to substitute *themselves*. They are told to watch those guys who start—to look for a slow step, a missed block, or a technical mess-up and to replace the guilty party, knowing that when he hits the sidelines, he'll be watching *your* every move.

Align Your Best Blockers According To Defensive Set

With the previous tip implemented, this valuable tactic is possible. If we play someone who plays an even defensive front, we move our best blockers to guard. If they play an odd front, we play our best blockers at tackle.

Set Your Offense To Set Their Defense

I have observed the play cards held on the sidelines by the professional coaches on Sunday afternoon and noticed that they resemble a rough draft of *Gone With the Wind.* I was amazed at the number of plays and sets that these teams employed and often wondered how they could run so much offense—until I remembered that their players don't have to study for a world history exam or do five pages of math homework every night. They study football day and night, and their multi-million-dollar paycheck depends on how well they learn the contents of that play card and how well they perform what is on it. I realized years ago that it wasn't how much *I* knew that would win games but how much those eleven fellows on the field knew. I would go into each game with twelve or fifteen running plays and maybe that many pass plays. We would name our blocks and teach them to the linemen by their names, and with any new plays, all we had to tell the linemen was the name of the block we were going to use with that particular play. What we *did* have was a simple means to position ourselves into any set we could imagine. With this system we could dictate with our sets what defense the opponent would be in and what technique our linemen would be blocking. With this scheme we were able to establish a game plan designed to attack the predicted defensive look. We also gave the other coach credit, realizing that he might not line up as we anticipated. Therefore, we had an audible system that our quarterback could use with one or two plays designed to go against *any* defense.

Have an In-Depth Scouting Report Against Best Opponents

Look for these *little things* that might give you an edge: Does the fullback lead ninety percent of plays? Do they run mostly toward *their* sidelines? Do the offensive linemen tip off plays by their stance? Does the QB lock up on the receiver? Does the stance of the backs tip off plays? Where do the backs/linemen look on the way to the line of scrimmage? Do line splits tip off plays? What plays/defenses hurt them in their previous games? Were any substitutions made in previous games because of injuries? Who is their "go to" back/lineman? Do you know your opponents well enough to anticipate any change they will make according to what you plan to do? (This goes back to the section on "Scout Yourself." Prepare a game plan according to what you would do if *you* were playing *you*.)

Don't Be So Proud That You Can't—or Won't—Learn from Other Coaches

"Other coaches" includes those at any level. I have picked up valuable information from ninth grade coaches and even those who coach at the middle school level. Usually these fellows have to implement their programs with much less equipment and assistance than those of us in larger programs; consequently, they must devise innovative measures that can help you and your program be more productive. In a previous section of this book, I discussed the means by which we obtain wisdom—"through years of trial and error or through the proven experience of others." Let me expand on that to include the *mistakes* of other coaches as well. If I stand and watch a guy put his hand on a hot stove, and he jerks it away with a blister on his palm exclaiming, "That's hot!" I don't have to touch that same stove to know that *it is hot!* Even bad coaches can teach you something. Good or bad, you should learn from the successes or mistakes of other coaches.

Don't Outsmart Yourself

Clinics are good—but don't come back home and try to implement everything you have in your notebook. You don't have the luxury of recruiting all over the country as those guys who speak at these clinics do. We try to pick up at least two or three things: a drill, a play, or it might be something as simple as changing terminology. When we tell the kids that "This is Alabama's or Auburn's or (you fill in the blank) drill (or play)," they may not be doing much that is different from what they are doing now, but because it is *this* college's drill or play, they get all "gung ho" and will put more emphasis on it.

Part VII

Developing a Simple, Effective, and Flexible Game Plan

Chapter 7

Scouting Your Opponent

Personal Observation

Before you begin to develop any game plan, it is essential that you exhaust every scouting tool you have available. I'm sure that there are some teams on your schedule that you know almost as much about as you do your own. Years ago, I heard Lou Holtz at a clinic, while speaking on this portion of coaching, declare that he wanted to know "what brand of toothpaste they brushed with every morning." I have always enjoyed going through a detailed description of my next opponent's last game over a cup of coffee on Saturday morning. There were times this was not possible due to the lack of coaches or scouts. One year, I had hired a fired-up rookie coach who wanted to learn every phase of the coaching profession. We had an important game coming up with a very good rival, one that I had played for years, and I probably could have given you the birthday and license-plate number of every player on the team. I decided to send this young man to scout them at their home game the next Friday night, some sixty miles away. On Thursday night I had him over for supper, and we had a clinic on the finer points of scouting. "Get there early so you can watch them warm-up....Take a stopwatch and time their snapper and their punter....Time how long the punt stays in the air....See how well their backup quarterback throws the football....Do any of the running backs throw the football?" I must have covered every facet of the game with him that night, and he copied down every word I said in his notebook. I instructed him to be at my place again on Saturday morning around six, and I'd feed him breakfast. At six o'clock sharp the next Saturday, as I was sitting at the kitchen table X-ing and O-ing and enjoying my third cup of coffee, I heard the expected knock on the door. This eager young coach walked through the door and handed me a notebook with a look on his face as if he were giving me the secret for curing cancer. I started flipping through the pages and could tell that the construction of this report must have continued almost until his knock on the door. Every detail was carefully noted—like the direction of the wind and even the numbers and names of the players that *didn't* dress out but were standing on the sidelines in their game jerseys. Every play they ran was diagrammed with the down, distance, and field position clearly shown—I had taught him well! I quickly turned every page, and as I tossed the notebook on the kitchen table, I gave my appraisal of our next week's opponent: "Just as I thought—they ain't changed a thing." I'm sure this swift assessment was somewhat of a letdown to my weary assistant, but the scouting report told me exactly what I needed to know. It made my game preparation almost complete. Realizing that this longtime foe was more than likely thinking the same about me, we changed our game plan just enough to throw off his analysis and to present him with a few surprises for next Friday night.

Films/Tapes

In the past five decades, scouting has evolved from waiting until three o'clock in the morning at the film lab for the 16mm reproduction of that night's game to viewing the outcome with the assistant coaches only minutes after the final whistle blows. In the old days we were lucky to obtain a discernible copy of our opponent's game film by Tuesday or Wednesday of the week of the game. Most of us had to show it to our booster club first, and, of course, there was *only* one copy. I will say this: When we *did* get those two canisters in our hands, all the coaches would gather in our "film room" (usually the living room at my house) and dissect each play with the command over and over again to the coach holding the "magic button"—"Run that back." Now, with modern technology, each coach can have a copy of only that part of the game that relates to his particular responsibility. Even with all of this modern technology, breaking down your opponent still involves many hours of tedious searching for that one small detail that will give you the necessary edge on Friday night. After we do the obvious—diagram each play and adjust the blocking against our defense—we look for tendencies. Do they run series? Do they script the first series? Are they predictable on certain downs—always run on first down, pass on third and long? If they are a running team, what percentage of the plays does the fullback lead? Who is their "go to" player? Who are their *best* players—lineman, receiver, linebacker, defensive back? Who are their weakest? We want to check the quarterback's arm. Can they beat you with the long ball? Is he consistent in the short-passing game?

On defense we look to see if their adjustments to certain sets produce weaknesses that we can take advantage of with our basic plays run from those sets. This again goes back to a system that has the flexibility that will allow you to adjust your game plan to exploit these weaknesses. We constantly look for a mismatch that will give us an edge, either on their defensive line or in their secondary. I've always said that you can't hide a weak player—yours or ours. The same is true about that special "hoss" that everybody knows and who will probably play on weekends the last part of his career. If you line up one of these "animals" at defensive tackle, we won't waste one of our better players on him. We always try to have someone who may not have the size and strength to do battle with this all-state candidate but who has the determination and courage to perform an operation that we call "frogging him." His responsibility in this particular game plan is to line up head-on this "havoc-wreaker" and to submarine his legs on every play. We figure that he can't make many tackles lying in a heap on top of our "frog." We apply this same philosophy to our receivers and to your secondary personnel. If one of your defensive backs is obviously superior to the rest, we adjust our sets and plays to make sure that he covers a decoy all night. At times, in order to accomplish this, we employ motion, or we shift to a set that isolates this gentleman on one of our less-talented receivers.

Newspaper Articles/Visits

The most difficult opponent to get information on is the new team that appears early on your schedule that has a new coach. Although this is a rare occurrence, it has happened to me more than once, and it is a situation that requires special preparation. You might be surprised what you can learn on Saturday morning at the local coffee shop on the square in the town of that new opponent. I've learned a lot sitting at a table (being sure that I don't wear a ball cap or tee shirt with my team logo on it) sipping on a cup of coffee, munching on a doughnut, and reading a copy of the morning paper. I've listened to the town's Saturday morning quarterbacks discuss everything from the bruised knee of their stud linebacker and the sprained ankle of their star running back to that special defense this new guy is running. There are other interesting little tidbits of information that you can pick up (while in disguise) that can be very helpful in devising your game plan for this fresh new foe. That newspaper I mentioned can also be helpful since most towns' aspiring sports writers often write more than the "ol' coach" would like for them to say. I have always subscribed to the newspapers from the towns of my top four or five toughest opponents just so I can keep track of them throughout the year. Of course, you young coaches who are "computer savvy" can now pull that information up daily with the simple click of a button.

Phone Calls

Throughout my personal life, I've always found it natural to be a friend to everyone. Someone important once told me, "You can never have too many friends." This statement is never truer than to someone in the coaching profession in which friends are a necessity. At each place I've coached, I've made it a policy to make friends with every coach in the surrounding vicinity. I have found these coaching buddies to be very beneficial in certain situations when some of my opposing coaches were somewhat less than cooperative when it comes to information-sharing. I'm sure that we all have received tapes that look as if they were filmed in the middle of a snowstorm or that the fellow shooting the game was told to save as much tape as possible, resulting in the play's being half over before you see anything. I'm not saying that these guys would intentionally do anything questionable, but I'm willing to bet that *their* coaches didn't try to *grade* what they sent *us*. In these situations, a phone call to their last opponent may answer questions not revealed on your TV screens or DVD players.

I recall a particular game back in the '60s when we were playing a team in Birmingham for the first time whose coach was notorious for concealing information. For some reason we didn't send a scout to watch them, so about all we knew about them was that they threw the ball a lot and had a pretty decent quarterback.

Finally, on Tuesday, I was able to contact one of those friends I mentioned who had played this team the previous week. He was showing the game film to his boosters that night but agreed to allow me and one of my coaches to come to his place on Wednesday night to view the film. After practice on Wednesday, we made the trip and arrived at his dressing room around seven o'clock. He had the film but had failed to mention that the game was played in a driving rainstorm. About all we saw of this hotshot quarterback was his slipping and sliding in three inches of mud, and the game ended in a nothing to nothing tie. We were able to see at least what defense they ran and what sets they used on offense. We made the necessary adjustments to our game plan on Thursday and made the hundred-mile trip the next day, stopping at a restaurant on the outskirts of Birmingham for a prearranged pre-game meal. I mention the meal to alert you young coaches to one more coaching tip: Don't trust a bunch of hungry athletes in a fine restaurant during a pre-game meal. Lack of communication between the coaches (who mistakenly sat in a separate room) and restaurant personnel, plus some flattering words from a good-looking bunch of young athletes to an obliging waitress, produced an overabundance of thick, greasy dinner rolls three and a half hours before kickoff. When we got to the field, we quickly found out that refusing to swap films wasn't the only trick this coach had up his sleeve. It was obvious that he knew more about *us* than we knew about *him*. Our main attack that year was a very quick scat back who was known for his ability to cut on a dime and give you six cents change. When we took the field for warm-ups, our shoes disappeared in the grass that looked as if it hadn't been cut since spring training. With that little hindrance to our stud running back and with a group of sluggish, overfed linemen, we were lucky to come out on top by five points with them on our eighteen-yard line when the horn sounded. Oh, yeah, that *pretty decent* quarterback—he certainly *was!* He threw for nearly three hundred yards against us and four years later was awarded the Heisman Trophy as the best football player in America.

Part VIII

Defensive Fundamentals of the Game

Chapter 8

Defensive Philosophy

Stunting

In the early years of my coaching career, I employed a one-gap, stunting-type defense on almost every down. Each defensive player was assigned a certain gap, and they would move to the specified gap on the snap. I found that stunting gave the less physical defensive linemen an advantage over their more physical opponents.

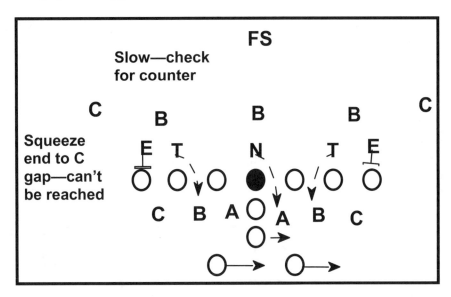

Figure 8–1 5–3 Tackles Pinch

In addition to this obvious reason, I stunted for the following four reasons: First, I stunted to stop the "jump through." What I mean by this is that we didn't want any uncovered lineman to have a clear shot at our linebackers. As I mentioned above, on every stunt called, each player has a definite gap responsibility. I like to run an odd front, which leaves the two guards uncovered. Depending on the particular stunt called, the nose man and one or the other or both tackles slant and are responsible for keeping the guards from having a "jump through" to our linebackers. This enables our linebackers to run free and to make tackles. I also stunted to confuse blocking schemes. When I hear coaches declare that they are going to line up in one defense and learn to play it well, I try to get *them* on my schedule. If you play me, you're going to have to prepare for at least three different looks on defense and from those looks up to forty variations. When coaches tell me that it's not possible to teach high school kids that much stuff, my only reply is, "Maybe not, but

I've done it for over fifty years!" If my just *telling* the coach about it confuses *him*, imagine what the *reality* of it does to a sixteen or seventeen-year-old offensive lineman. In addition, besides the confusion aspect of stunting and freeing up linebackers, stunting also allows you to put pressure on the offense that likes to throw the football. Most teams that *do* throw the ball a lot do so because their quarterback is pretty good at it. If you allow a well-trained quarterback time to go through his reads, he'll complete passes. If you can lock up and play man for just a few steps, that same quarterback has to look for his "hot route" with your best defensive players breathing down his neck. Finally, part of my stunt package is what I call "jitterbugging." Some coaches call it "stemming," but regardless of your terminology, it prevents or severely hampers your opponent's ability to audible at the line of scrimmage by changing the alignment of the defensive linemen and/or linebackers before the snap. As I mentioned, I go into each game with at least three different defensive sets with the ability to move quickly from one set to another and to stunt from the last look we give you. So, what you *see* may not be what you *get!* This is especially confusing to a group of teenage linemen who have only six days to work against it.

This one-gap, stunting-type defense worked well unless I was playing "myself." What really hurts the one-gap defense is the "block down—kick out" type offense. With good vertical splits and the proper first step, stunts can be picked up and running lanes produced as illustrated in the basic off-tackle play below:

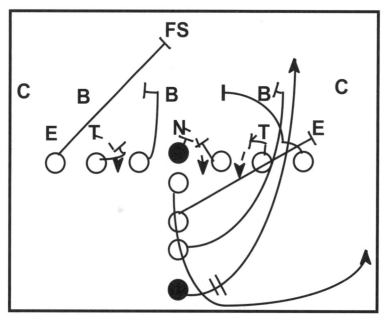

Figure 8–2 Off-Tackle Play

As in all aspects of football, personnel *should* dictate what you do both offensively and defensively. I emphasize the word *should* because there are still stubborn coaches who are going to run the same thing every year despite personnel. I have always enjoyed nature. I like to hunt, to fish, and in recent years just to walk (or to ride) around in a "big pasture," chasing a little white ball. If you do these things, you notice that the scenes of nature are constantly changing with the times. I firmly believe that the same should be true of the high school coach. Not only must you change with the times but with what nature (Mama and Daddy) gives you. I'll emphasize again—we don't have a million- dollar recruiting budget and access to great athletes all over the country suited to our particular schemes. Let me say this though: If you have been at a school for any length of time and have been lucky and successful enough to secure the confidence and control of the entire football community, you probably *can* develop players who will enable you to run the same stuff year-in and year-out.

Triangular Read

As the years went by and my knowledge of the game expanded, I learned to better adjust my defense to the personnel I had developed. I learned that if I could line up with decent (or better), good-sized defensive linemen, I could win with smaller linebackers if I taught the linemen to read *two* gaps. During those years that I had smaller defensive linemen, and I was able to compensate with bigger linebackers—I was *still* good. If I had both big, agile defensive linemen and big, quick linebackers—I was *fantastic!* I continued to develop the multiple-gap defensive theory until, after many hours of off-season drills, I worked my defense into a three-gap read that, when run correctly, freed the best tacklers on the team (the linebackers) to make tackles. Later in my career, although I still worked on stunts every day, I worked more on this Triangular-Read technique illustrated in Figure 8–3:

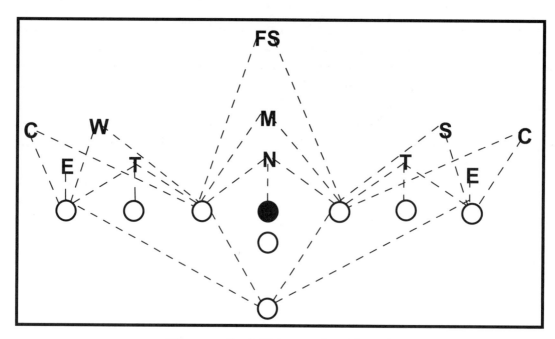

Figure 8–3 Triangular Read

<u>Nose</u>—Key on center and both guards.

<u>Tackles</u>—Key on guard, tackle, and end.

<u>Ends</u>—Key on offensive end to near back.

<u>Mike LB</u>—Key through guard to fullback.

<u>Sam LB</u>—Key on offensive end and offensive guard.

<u>Will LB</u>—If the end is gone, key on uncovered lineman. Primary responsibility is pass and pursuit.

<u>Defensive backs</u>—Key through guards to fullback.

*If the scouting report indicates that guards lead 90% of the plays, we change our keys to compensate.

The following illustration gives you the idea of this technique we use to stop the traditional Wing-T offense's favorite plays with our 5-3 Triangular-Read defense:

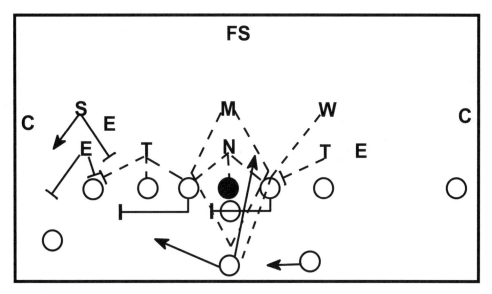

Figure 8-4 5-3 Triangular-Read

Nose—Triangular Read—Key on center and both guards.

Strong Tackle— Triangular Read with emphasis on guard and tackle—Primary read is the tackle and right guard, depending on the scouting report.

Mike LB—Primary read is through the guard to the FB.

Willie LB—Same as Mike.

Sam LB—Same as Mike.

(Passing situation: I go to Dime and replace DT with DB.)

Stopping Certain Popular Plays with a 5–3 Triangular Read

When I had adequate personnel and the techniques were played correctly, I had success with the Triangular-Read defense against some very potent offenses. As I have mentioned, all of my eggs were never put into one basket, and every game preparation included at least three different defenses with several looks on each. I have shown how we worked our Triangular Read against the traditional Wing-T plays. On the following pages I'll show the coaching techniques that we employed against these six most popular running plays:

1. Trap

2. Lead Play

3. Zone/ Zone Read

4. Power

5. Sweep

6. Inside Veer

EVEN TRAP

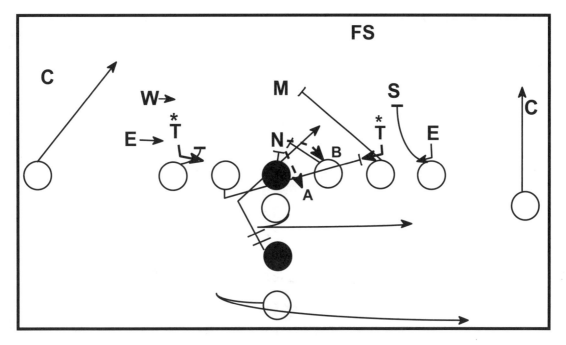

Figure 8–5 Even Trap

Will—Slide and look for reverse or bootleg.

Mike—Clean-up man—We like to stop trap without using Mike.

Sam—Slide and look for option, reverse, or bootleg.

Weak End—Slide and look for reverse or bootleg.

Both Tackles—Step with inside foot—Shoot hands to control offensive tackle—Flatten him—Go no farther than the center.

Nose—Small, quick nose (A)—fill gap. Big, strong nose (B)—whip guard.

Strong End—Stay in front of TE and look for trap option or inside veer. If end blocks down, jam him—Can't be reached or kicked out.

LEAD

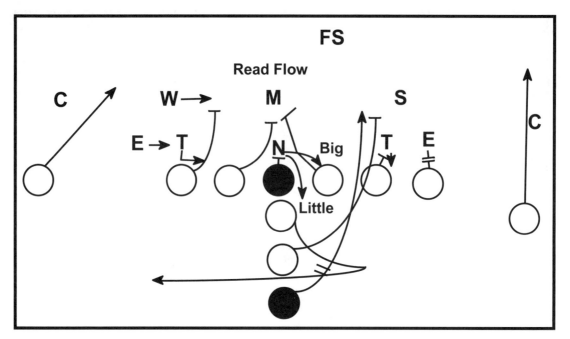

Figure 8-6 Lead

<u>Will</u>—Slide and look for reverse or bootleg.

<u>Mike</u>—Read flow—Play through block with backside shoulder.

<u>Sam</u>—Take on blocker with inside shoulder.

<u>Weak End</u>—Slide and look for reverse or bootleg.

<u>Weak Tackle</u>—Step with inside foot—Shoot hands to control offensive tackle—Flatten him—Go no farther than center. If the guard blocks down, the play is either a trap or lead—Study the offensive guard's release on film to determine which.

<u>Nose</u>—Must be double-teamed! Little nose—fill gap. Big nose—whip guard.

<u>Strong Tackle</u>—If tackle tries to man-block me, if I can't whip him—Frog him (cut him).

<u>Strong End</u>—Jam end—Can't be turned out.

ZONE

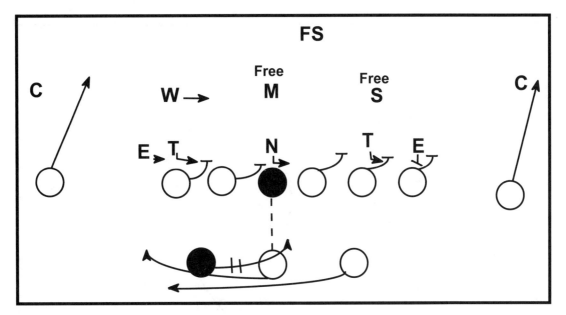

Figure 8-7 Zone

Will—Slide—Play slow—Has pitch on the option.

Mike—Should be free to play behind the runner—Look for cutback.

Sam—Should not be touched—Make tackle.

Weak End—Slide—Has QB on the option.

Weak Tackle—Step with inside foot—Shoot hands to control offensive tackle—Flatten him—Go no farther than center.

Nose—Whip center—Keep him off Mike.

Strong Tackle—Flatten tackle—Stay on the LOS.

Strong End—Can't be reached.

POWER

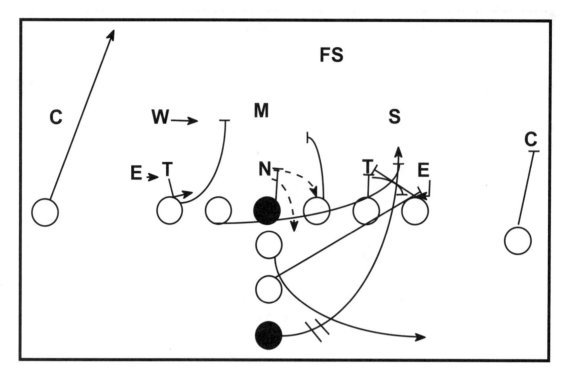

Figure 8–8 Power

<u>Will</u>—Slide and look for reverse, bootleg, or cutback.

<u>Mike</u>—Should be free to read flow and to make the tackle.

<u>Sam</u>—Slide and attack blocker with inside shoulder.

<u>Weak End</u>—Slide and look for reverse or bootleg.

<u>Weak Tackle</u>—Step with inside foot—Shoot hands to control offensive tackle—Flatten him—Go no farther than center.

<u>Nose</u>—If little nose—fill gap. If big nose—whip guard. Right guard can't be allowed to release.

<u>Strong Tackle</u>—Aggressively attack tight end—Create a pile.

<u>Strong End</u>—Stay in front of tight end—If end blocks down, jam him and keep shoulders parallel to the LOS and take on blocker—Can't be turned out.

SWEEP

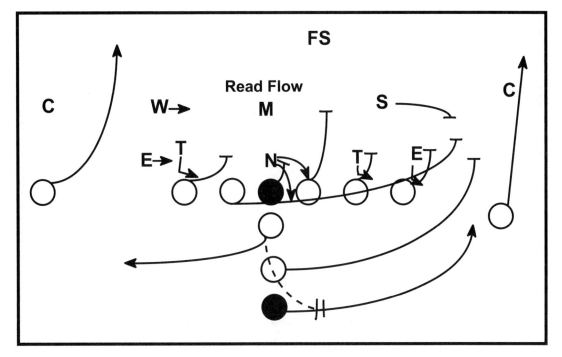

Figure 8–9 Sweep

<u>Will</u>—Slide and look for reverse, bootleg, or cutback.

<u>Mike</u>—Read flow—Play ball inside-out.

<u>Sam</u>—If guard turns up, play him with inside shoulder.

<u>Weak End</u>—Slide and look for reverse or bootleg.

<u>Weak Tackle</u>—Step with inside foot—Shoot hands to control offensive tackle—Flatten him—Go no farther than center.

<u>Nose</u>—If little nose—fill gap. If big nose–whip guard. Guard does not get out.

<u>Strong Tackle</u>—Can't be reached—Play down the LOS.

<u>Strong End</u>—Can't be reached—Turn play inside.

INSIDE VEER

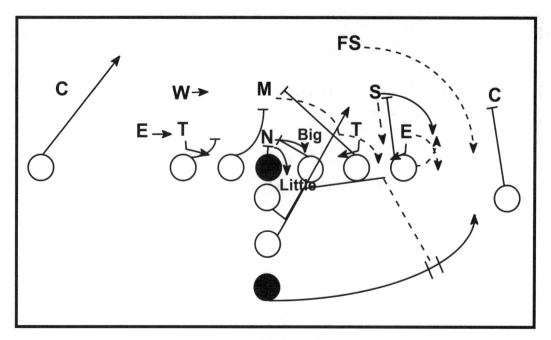

Figure 8–10 Inside Veer

<u>Will</u>—Slide and look for reverse or bootleg.

<u>Mike</u>—Slow read—Should be free to help with dive—To QB—To pitch.

<u>Sam</u>— If tight end blocks down, Sam has QB to pitch along with FS. If tight end releases, Sam takes dive.

<u>Weak End</u>—Slide and look for reverse or bootleg.

<u>Weak Tackle</u>—Step with inside foot—Shoot hands to control offensive tackle—Flatten him—Go no farther than center.

<u>Nose</u>—Little nose—fill gap. Big nose—whip guard.

<u>Strong Tackle</u>—Step with inside foot—Shoot hands to control offensive tackle and make tackle.

<u>Strong End</u>— If tight end blocks down, squeeze. If tight end releases, play pitch along with FS.

Special Defenses

In game preparation (especially against our toughest opponents), I'm *not* going to let you beat me with your five or six best plays. I figure that if I can stop those plays that you work on ninety percent of the time, you aren't going to beat me with those that you work on only ten percent of the time. I've inserted a couple of examples of my "special defenses" to stimulate thinking and to show what can be taught in a short amount of time with consistent terminology and techniques. Earlier I mentioned we sometimes named certain plays and defenses after successful teams. The first example is a defense we called "Dallas" after "America's Team," the Dallas Cowboys—a very successful team at the time we installed it. We ran this defense along with our other looks in the state-championship game. In that game our Mike linebacker made eighteen tackles, and we beat a very good football team, stymieing their very potent offense with these new wrinkles:

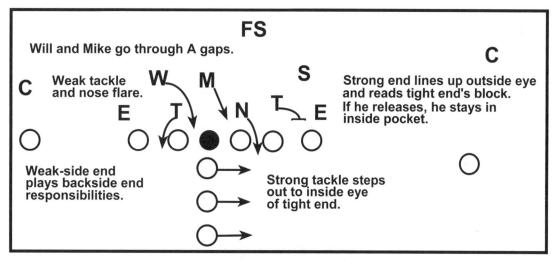

Figure 8–11 Dallas Strong

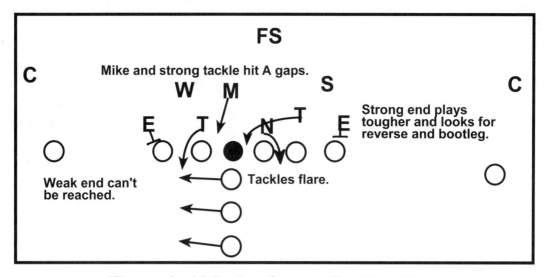

Figure 8–12 Dallas Strong, Tackles Flare

If the other coach had a game plan that hurt any particular one of the defenses we had prepared, I *always* had a backup. The following defensive alignments were some I used against certain sets and certain plays:

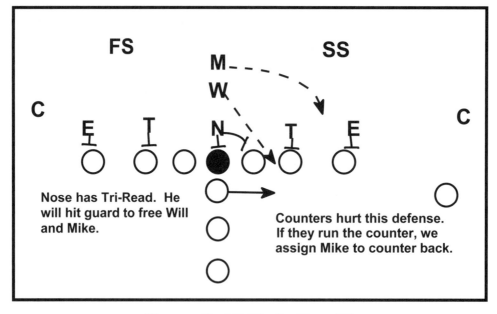

Figure 8–13 Bird's Eye 50

Defensive Fundamentals 75

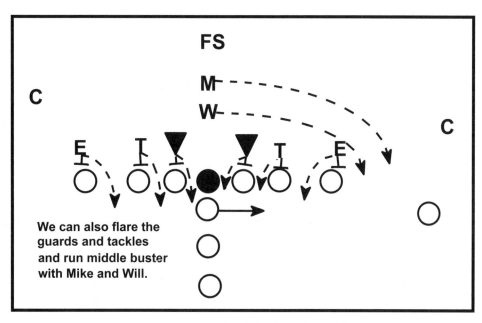

Figure 8–14 Bird's Eye 60

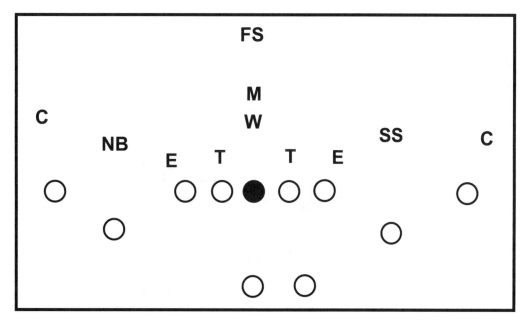

Figure 8–15 Bird's Eye 44

This was a very successful defense against the spread-offensive sets that I saw in my later years. We ran a variety of stunts, including those shown with the other sets. With special personnel, we would run man-and-one in the secondary.

5–3 Variations

I have always liked the 5–3 defense against any set that is designed primarily to run the football. I have shown one variation we used—the Triangular Read—that was very effective when we had the personnel to run it correctly. I soon discovered if the offensive linemen thought that we were lining up and reading, they would hunker down and explode off the football, trying to stalemate our defender with a power block. With big, strong offensive linemen, this would seem to be the answer to our read defense, but as I have said, with me—what you *see* is not always what you *get!* The 5–3 also lends itself to several stunt packages, which of course I developed to complement the Tri-Read. After a big offensive tackle blasts off on our defensive tackle and gets a plus on that play, he gets cocky. On the next play, if we are stunting off the same defensive look, he will explode on air, and then our man is sitting in your backfield. A confused blocker is usually not an effective one.

I will insert just a few of the stunts that we ran from our 5–3. The type of stunt we ran depended upon scouting report, down and distance, and game tendencies.

5–3 Stunt Package

Three types of slants that I taught are flat, cut, and penetrating.

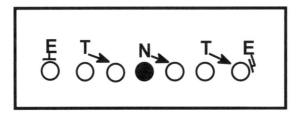

Figure 8–16 Flat Slant

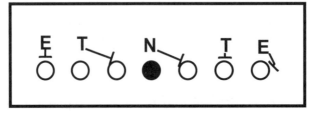

Figure 8–17 Cut Slant

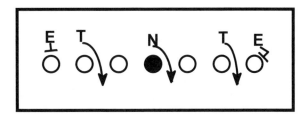

Figure 8–18 Penetrating Slant

The type of slant that we used varied with what we wanted to accomplish according to the opponent's tendencies and personnel. For example, if their tendency was to run toward the wide side or as some coaches do, *their* bench, we would have a flat slant called in that direction. Whether we had a two-man slant or a three-man slant was usually decided by the opponent's play preference and down and distance. We used the cut technique when we wanted to keep the guards off the linebackers. If we expected a pass, we liked the penetrating slant—usually with the linebackers hitting opposite holes. Below are only a few of the blitzes that we used off the 5–3:

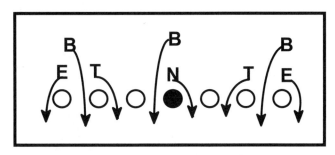

Figure 8–19 Eight-Man Blitz

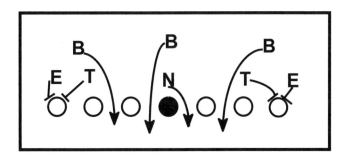

Figure 8–20 Middle Blitz—Tackles Cut Ends

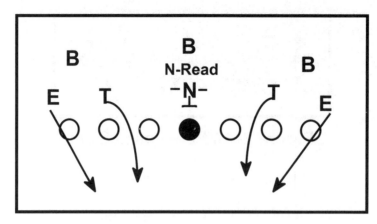

Figure 8–21 Tackles Pinch

I have given only a few examples of the defensive looks that I have used through the last fifty-plus years of coaching. I enjoy coaching defense and will usually have two or three looks that I develop that could be called unconventional, but I assure you that they are sound for what they are designed to stop. I always figured that the more defensive looks that I could give my opposition to work on, the less offense those coaches could prepare for me to stop.

Chapter 9

Selection of Personnel

Defensive Linemen

In my later years during the off-season, I would let the younger coaches handle the agility drills and weight program, and I worked mainly with my defensive-line techniques (without pads of course). I worked on defense *first and foremost.* As coaches you must never forget that *you win ball games on defense!* As with all of our players, we like our defensive linemen to be able to physically whip anyone he may line up against. Also, as with most high school teams (or at any level), this is not always going to be the case. For this reason, we equip our defensive down-linemen with several different techniques that they can use to defeat the blockers as well as the blocking schemes. We begin with the defensive stance. Since we stunt as well as read, we make sure that the down-linemen mix up their stances. We work on their coming hard on their stunts from either a three-point or a four-point stance. The same holds true when they are reading. We want to make sure that the alert offensive coach doesn't get a tip-off from our stance that shows him what defense we are running.

I start by showing them where I want their heads, their hands, and their feet. I teach them this in each of the defensive techniques they will be playing—head-up, outside eye, and inside eye. I never work on all techniques on the same day until I make sure that they have mastered each one. In our read defense, we can't crowd the line of scrimmage. This gives the offensive player an advantage because it creates blocking angles, especially in an inside-eye or outside-eye technique where they are blocked by alignment if they crowd the line of scrimmage. Also, with the deeper alignment, our tackle can get a piece of the tight end and keep him off the linebacker if that is where his read takes him. If the guard pulls away, this alignment, with a good read, will keep him from being cut off by the offensive tackle. We tell the defensive lineman to hit—*in the teeth*—whichever offensive lineman the read directs him to—which stops the lineman's initial momentum. We want him to be aware of where the offensive player's feet are, to stay low, and to control him on the line of scrimmage with his hands and legs. After we make contact and control the blocker with our hands, we must disengage and locate the football. We don't want our defensive player to push the blocker into the backfield since this will create running lanes.

In modern-day football the *hands* have become an integral part of both offensive and defensive-line play. The rule change for offensive linemen in the late '80s makes it difficult sometimes to determine who is on offense and who is on defense. Many times the line of scrimmage resembles a heavy-weight-boxing match with both sides vying for hand position. Because of this, we insist that all our athletes do a regiment of fingertip pushups and reverse dips every day as part of their strength training.

Now this next statement may sound cruel to all of you mamas who are reading this book. Another thing I tell them is to come off the ball at the first of the game and try to hurt the guys in front of them. I have found that this tends to make the offensive linemen overly aggressive and helps my defensive linemen use their pass-rushing techniques more effectively. We also work on these techniques in the off-season. They include the power rush, the inside twist, the outside twist, and the swim technique.

Another consideration one must recognize while coaching the defensive line is one of simple physics. If I have to line up a 190-pound defensive tackle in front of your 275-pound offensive lineman, he's in trouble if he has to do that "control stuff" we talked about. I go back to that old axiom "low man wins" and tell him to cut him (we call it "frog him") to create a pile. If this is the case, we adjust the rest of our defensive strategy to compensate. I have already stated that I want my best lineman on the center. It has been my observation through the years that most coaches play their slowest man at center, and I've always said that on "Hike," he becomes a one-armed man. A good player on the nose can generate much havoc on most offensive schemes and can also disrupt the center-quarterback exchange—creating fumbles.

Defensive Ends

We have three rules for our defensive ends. They are very obvious and simple, but they take hours of drilling to perfect. The end works from a two-point stance, keeping his butt in the chute and his shoulders parallel, and we tell him, "Don't get reached, don't get turned out, and don't get blown off the ball." What I'm really saying is that he can't be blocked—period! Ideally, this primary-perimeter player is one-third defensive back, one-third linebacker, and one-third down-lineman. The defensive end's task in any defensive alignment is a very difficult one. He must squeeze the off-tackle play, contain the sweep and zone stretch, give us an outside rush on the passer, and in some alignments play pass coverage. While performing all of that, he is blocked with guards, tackles, fullbacks, wingbacks, and ends. He also has different responsibilities on the inside and outside veer. I heard the offensive coordinator of a major college team say at a clinic one year that he wanted to initiate the "windshield-wiper effect" in the defensive ends they played. He then demonstrated that statement by turning his head back and forth like a windshield wiper. In other words, he wanted to have the ends thinking and therefore confused on every play. Most of us know that in high-speed sports such as football, the players don't have time to do much thinking—they must react! I work with the defensive ends on the mats during the off-season, reading through the offensive end to the nearest back and showing him how to defeat the various blocking schemes that he will face. The defensive end's alignment depends on two things: the defense called and his size and strength. If I have a strong defensive end and I'm in a read defense, I back him off the line a step to give him more time to read the offensive end's first move. If we are in a slant defense and the tackle is slanting away from him, just before the snap, I have him move tighter to the line and nose up on the offensive end. In this technique the defensive end knows that he has to squeeze the off-tackle hole and keep the tight end off the linebacker. If the slant is toward him, he can loosen because the tackle will assume off-tackle responsibilities. If we have a smaller, weaker defensive end, we *never* slant the tackle away from him. By the time we start spring training, the entire defensive team must know every defensive technique that we will employ.

Linebackers

"*AG-ile, MO-bile, and HOS-tile*"— I first heard these terms at a coaching clinic many years ago from the linebacker coach at **Penn State University** in describing the attributes they look for in the linebackers they recruit. My philosophy has always been that not only does it take a special athlete to play this position, but it also takes a special coach to coach it. Coaching a good linebacker is somewhat like coaching a running back who averages one hundred yards a game or a punter who is averaging forty-five yards per kick. *DON"T!!* I can recall in my early "know it all" years of coaching having kids that could kick the football into the lower stratosphere and have it come down forty or fifty yards downfield. The *problem* was that they weren't holding the ball properly, and their drop needed to be worked on. After I straightened out these obvious deficiencies, their efforts usually dropped down to a line drive that traveled about thirty or forty yards. *"If it ain't broke, don't fix it!"* This very familiar axiom needs to be written on a large sign and hung in every coach's office in the country. The three adjectives used by the Penn State coach in describing what they looked for in players they wanted for this position can be interpreted by any old country boy as "*quick, fast, and mean.*" Throw in *big,* and if that young man can read and write, he'll be getting letters not only from that school but also from many others.

As all coaches know, weekends are never long enough to do all that we have to do in preparation for Monday. When we break down the film of the next opponent, we like to have our linebackers and free safety (who calls secondary coverage) there breaking them down with the coaches. It is as imperative that these gentlemen know the complete defensive scheme as it is for your quarterback to know what everyone does on every play on offense.

We go over with them how we intend to stop their favorite plays and what stunts or alignments are necessary against certain offensive sets. We tell our linebackers that they need to play as if they are tied together with a string, and we drill every day on the proper angles they must take on certain calls and defensive alignments. But, let me emphasize again—don't *over-coach* them. When the quarterback says, "Hike," they must *react*—they won't have time to *think*.

Over the years most of my defensive schemes were developed for the linebacker to make a majority of the tackles. This philosophy put a premium on finding that *special* player to play this *special* position. The linebacker's role on defense is as important as the quarterback's role is to the offense, and in many cases even more so. Linebackers are not only responsible for their alignment, but also they are ultimately responsible for the alignment of their teammates. Linebackers are asked to make several pre-snap calls and adjustments based on the offensive formation, personnel, location on the field, and down and distance. As offensive football continues to evolve and change into more "spread" formations that utilize players with more athletic ability, the linebacker, more than any other position, has been asked to assume more and more responsibilities. A linebacker is asked to be a physical player, capable of defeating the block of a 270-pound offensive tackle, while on the very next play, he may be assigned to cover a speedy slot receiver on a smash route. These responsibilities require an efficient linebacker to be quick on his feet, good with his hands, fearless in his heart, and a leader by nature. Along with all of these duties, let us not forget that, yes, he is still expected to make *most* of the tackles. Some of these traits can be refined through hours of grueling practice while others are simply God given. The qualities needed to be a successful linebacker make this position unique and very special. It *must* be an honor to play linebacker! Notice that the qualities mentioned did NOT include having to run a 4.4-second 40-yard dash, bench pressing 350 pounds, or standing 6'2" tall. Many of the most productive and successful linebackers I have coached over the years weighed less than 160 pounds and, at best, had only average speed. These less-gifted players were not only *special* players but *special* people as well. They were people who knew how to take what God had given them and to turn every ounce of their potential into a valuable resource to the TEAM. This exceptional player is just one of many examples of why football is such a great game and a valuable springboard into life. **AG**-ile, **MO**-bile, and **HOS**-tile—plus **dedicated commitment**—what a great combination!

"Who was your best?" This question is always asked when coaches sit around and discuss certain positions and certain players. Replace *was* with *were* in that question, and it becomes easier to answer. I won't tell you about *all* of the outstanding linebackers that I have had the privilege of watching destroy the other teams' offenses, but I *will* tell you of the first one that always jumps into my mind following this question. He had many great games during his career, but the one I'll describe was typical. We were playing a big rival located only a few miles from our school. They had a very good running game, and I drew up a special defense to stop it. Of course, it involved the defensive abilities of our best linebacker. The diagram below shows the basic lineup that we used (and I'll admit that it looks like a major highway up the middle):

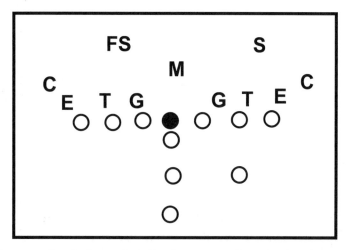

Figure 9–1 Special Defense—Stud Linebacker

This might have been the case but for one thing—that big **M** in the middle was our afore-mentioned linebacker, and *he* was a *Major roadblock*. He made twenty-two tackles that night, leading us to a hard-fought victory. After the game, a scout from a large university (who was there scouting the opponent's big running back) came to our dressing room to get information on this phenomenal linebacker who ruled the middle that night and held that big running back he was recruiting to under forty yards. The information that I gave him made his jaw drop in disbelief. "Coach, I hate to tell you," I said, "but he's just a ninth grader." If I had a ten-dollar bill for every tackle that fellow made in the four years that he lined up for me, I could've purchased a fairly decent car.

Defensive Backs (With Drills Used for Selection)

This position must consist of your best and smartest athletes. It is here where you can get beaten *in a hurry!* Confidence and the ability to communicate are two key factors in the selection process of secondary personnel. Not only must this player be *physically* tough, but also he must have the highest degree of *mental* toughness of any player on the defensive team. He must be able to shake off a pass completion and *immediately* prepare for the next play. Our first consideration, as we look for someone to play this position, is his ability to play man-to-man pass defense. Teams that can run the football force you into man-to-man coverage. Man coverage allows you to overload the zone in the latest offensive trend—zone blocking. I've said through the years that if I have *one* that can play man-to-man, I'll be *good*. If I can find *two*, I'm *real good!* Give me *three,* and I'm *bad!* If I have *four* guys who can play you man—I'm *real, real bad!* In order for a player to be able to play man coverage, this next statement is obvious: *he must be able to run and to run fast!* It is also obvious that he will be running backwards as he begins his coverage, but it is very important that you teach these players, through countless drills, how to properly run forward before you work on the backpedal procedure. The procedure for his stride and his hands and elbows is as important backwards as it is forward—pushing off his toes with his elbows in tight so that he can make quick lateral movements. In every game in any defensive alignment and against every offensive set, it is imperative that your defensive backs realize these five things: down and distance, field position, field condition, where their help is, and the score. We tell them that as the play begins to keep their eyes on the bottom of the receiver's numbers and to stay in the backpedal mode as long as possible to avoid being turned out of position. The cushion he keeps depends on several factors. The obvious are down and distance and the position on the field, but also a very important consideration will be the speed of the receiver compared to the speed of your D-back. Regardless, if this cushion diminishes to three to five yards, he needs to plant, turn and run, for if it gets less than three—he's beaten. We also drill on his closing the cushion when he sees the non-throwing hand of the quarterback leave the ball. Unless you are truly blessed with an abundance of exceptional personnel, at least one of these vital players is not going to have the necessary speed to hang with the quality receivers who play the game today. This being the case, realize that the safety position player need not be as fast—just very football savvy and a *sure tackler*. An overly aggressive safety trying to make a punishing linebacker-type tackle can cost you long yardage, touchdowns, and even ball games.

I've never played chess, but I do know the concept of winning in that game—anticipating your opponent's next move. The same cat-and-mouse game holds true in football. If you are successful in stopping the run with this defensive strategy, you had better be prepared to disguise or change your coverage. The *good* teams on your schedule *will* have an alternate plan.

The importance of a seasoned athlete at this position was forever impressed in my mind during a state-championship game in the late '60s. We were in the finals against a perennial powerhouse from Montgomery, playing them on their home field. We pulled out all the stops for this game. Our booster club chartered a plane to eliminate any possibility of travel fatigue, and we wanted our team to spend the night in their own beds and to eat their mama's cooking for breakfast. Let me insert here a little note of interest pertinent to the story. The plane we chartered was taking off from a brand-new airport that had been opened only a few days earlier. We also were taking a bus for those young players who (we thought) had no chance of playing. We planned to reward this young bunch with an all-you-can-eat buffet in Birmingham on the way down. Everything was working out well, but as Paul Harvey announces every day on his radio program, "Now...for the rest of the story" and to that brand-new airport and my reason for relating this story: our all-city defensive back. Although this young man was born and raised in Huntsville, he didn't have a clue where the new airport had been built. I failed to mention that I opted not to fly with the starters but rode in the young guys' bus to allow two of my assistants the opportunity to fly and to allow me to enjoy the all-you-can-eat buffet. The team met at the school and was told to drive to the airport where roll would be called on the plane. One of the assistants had a travel list to make sure all the team made it to the new facility. We had everything covered (we thought), but as the poet Robert Burns said in his poem "To a Mouse," "The best laid plans of mice and men often go awry." And awry they went! The bus left several hours before the rest of the team to allow for a much slower travel speed and, of course, the all-you-can-eat buffet. The remainder of the team later met at the school, formed a convoy, and headed for the airport. Our problems began as our defensive back was caught at a red light, separating him from the rest of the team. Then he made a wrong turn, heading *away* from the airport. The next problem we encountered was the dying of our old faithful team bus, the Green Goose, about forty miles north of Birmingham. As mentioned, we *were* voted the best-prepared team in the state, so we went to Plan B: calling one of the assistants and having him drive our other team bus to our breakdown point and then simply swapping rides and continuing on to Montgomery. The main difficulty we had with this was that we would be a couple of hours late for the buffet and the fact that *this* assistant had the travel list. The next dilemma we had to surmount was a strong cold front that was approaching North Alabama from the west that was about to collide with the unusually hot and humid air mass in our area. As often happens with these circumstances, tornadoes were expected to form ahead of this front. About the time the team was strapping on their seatbelts and preparing for takeoff, a tornado warning was issued for the Huntsville area. Almost simultaneously, the flight attendant announced to the coach on the plane that he had a phone call. Thinking that it was a booster wishing us good luck, coupled with the fact that a tornado was bearing down on them, the coach said, "Forget the phone call. Let's go." Of course, the phone call was from the all-city defensive back whose name was on the travel list in the pocket of the coach driving bus #2 on his way to pick up the group stranded north of Birmingham. At this point in time, *we* didn't realize that this young fellow was still in Huntsville, and *he* didn't realize that there would have been *at least* a hundred boosters who would've been glad to drive him to

Montgomery in plenty of time to line up in this all-important game. Not all was lost, however. We *did* make it to the buffet—and it *was* good! When the team made it to its resting area at a local high school, we had a message waiting for us concerning our stranded player. Had it not been for the very inclement weather, he could still have made it to the game since one of the boosters offered to fly him there in his private plane. Tornadoes are not something to challenge in a small aircraft. When toe met leather at 7:00 pm, we were minus our best defensive back who was listening to the game on the radio back in Huntsville. Two plays later, we were also minus our two starting offensive guards (one, also an all-state linebacker). Both of these guys were sitting on the bench with icepacks on their ankles. If you have coached for any length of time, you know that when adversity strikes, you don't have time to sit around and moan about it—you adjust. On this championship night, our adjustments were to line up our all-state running back at the safety position which had been vacated by the player at the red light back in Huntsville. The two offensive guards were quickly replaced by two of those sophomores who (we thought) had no chance of playing but enjoyed a six-hour bus ride and a pre-game meal consisting of an all-you-can-eat buffet. Our kids played hard, and with the tornado-like weather also in the Montgomery area, conditions were more conducive to our running attack than to our opponent's more pass-orientated offense. Needless to say, our running back, who was converted into a two-way player at kickoff and who had to slop through two inches of mud and water, did not have his best game. Despite all of these hardships, midway through the fourth quarter, we were locked up 0 to 0 with this powerhouse. Now, for the point of this story: we had to punt from our own forty-yard line, so we sent in our punt team to execute this important but usually routine assignment. (Here's one more insertion that I'm sure most of you will think that I'm making up.) This punter was yet *another* sophomore placed into this starting position four days before the game when our regular man had his nineteenth birthday, rendering him ineligible. The snap was perfect, his form was good. There was only one problem: he missed the ball! Suddenly, it was first and ten for our opponent from our thirty-yard line. On the first play, they lined up in a two-tight-wing-right formation, and the quarterback took a seven-step drop. The two tight ends ran takeoffs, and the wingback ran four yards upfield and then hit the hole down the middle toward our safety. This safety was our worn-out running back who had practiced a total of maybe fifteen minutes at this spot all week. An out-of-position and dead-tired safety watched as this wingback hit the corner of the end zone for the state-championship touchdown. Although we carried home the red trophy that night instead of the blue one, I can honestly say that I have *never* been any prouder of any bunch of kids in my entire coaching career.

Pass-Defense Drills

More games are either won or lost because of the performance of the young men who line up in our defensive backfield—good or bad. Included are some drills and coaching points that I have used throughout my career to aid in the selection of this very important position. After you decide on the personnel to play this position, it is important that you develop and consistently perform sound and significant drills. The drills must replicate as closely as possible game situations that the defender will encounter. As is true with any drill, in our pass-defense drills, we must stress the little things and accept nothing short of perfection in the execution of the fundamentals needed to effectively play this game-breaking position. I have shown only a few of the drills that we use during the course of a season, enough to stimulate the mind of the innovative coach to construct drills relevant to his particular situation. Most of these drills are as old as the game of football and did not originate with me but are still most successful in increasing the proficiency of the young player. I have always contended that the most successful coaches are those who have the imagination of a five-year-old child. These are the coaches who are able to project the reality of a game situation into meaningful drills on the practice field.

Footwork

In order for a player to become a good pass defender, it is imperative that he master the technique of running away from the LOS while looking through the receiver to the quarterback. Since this is not a natural running motion, we insist that our pass defenders perform some form of this drill every day. When these skills are developed and polished, all other aspects of playing this position well are greatly enhanced.

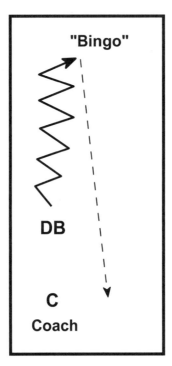

Figure 9–2 Pass Defender Drill

Coaching Points: The defender lines up five yards in front of and facing the coach. On command, the defender begins to run backwards, being careful **NOT** to backpedal. The coach controls his movement with a football held over his head—moved first one way and then the other. The first step is back at an angle, open, then crossover—left over right. With the movement of the ball, the defender plants his back foot, lowers his center of gravity, pivots, and rolls his hips as he changes direction. This action is all in a straight line, not zigzag. After the defender gains proficiency in this procedure, the coach will throw the ball, making sure that it is caught at its highest point and that he does not take an extra step. He must plant his back foot, yell "Bingo," and sprint back to the coach.

Man-to-Man

When we play man-to-man defense, we play as tight as we can without getting beaten. We match up our speed with their speed. If we are faster, we will get between them and the quarterback. If we cannot match speed, we have to give more ground to get more distance and play what we call "soft man-to-man." This means that we have to keep the receiver in front of us at all times. We want to put more people in the box than they can block when we run this defense.

When we begin this drill, we limit the routes the receiver runs to these four:
  1. Spot
  2. Square-in
  3. Square-out
  4. Takeoff

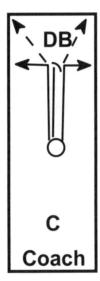

Figure 9–3 Man-to-Man Drill

Also in the first stages of the drill, we cover the routes without using a football. When we are satisfied that the proper techniques are being employed, we throw the football, looking for good position and playing the ball aggressively through the receiver. As the defender progresses, we add the out-and-up and the stop-and-go patterns.

Man-and-One

In this drill, we line up as we did on the man-to-man but add a safety behind the man coverage. We teach the safety to watch the eyes of the quarterback, and we tell him that when the ball is thrown—"It's yours!"

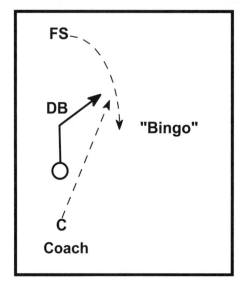

Figure 9–4 Man-and-One Drill

React and Score

I believe this to be one of the most important drills that we use. We want our defensive backs to possess a degree of confidence that borders on cockiness. We tell him that if the ball leaves the quarterback's hand—"He's throwing it to *you!*" In this drill, we line up anyone who is involved in pass defense, including the linebackers. We will line up in either Cover 2 or Cover 3 with the appropriate personnel. We place standup dummies at various places on the field to represent the receivers. The coach assumes the quarterback position in front of a complete backfield aligned in a variety of sets. The offense will use drop-back, sprint-out, play-action, and bootleg action in this drill. Rotation, alignment, adjustments, eye position, and reaction to the ball are components that can be observed in this drill. When the ball is thrown to one of the dummy receivers, we insist that *everyone* sprint to the ball. The nearest defender will get the Bingo, and the next nearest defender will throw a block on the dummy, taking out the most likely tackler. The rest of the defenders will sprint to get in front of the interceptor and lead him to a touchdown!

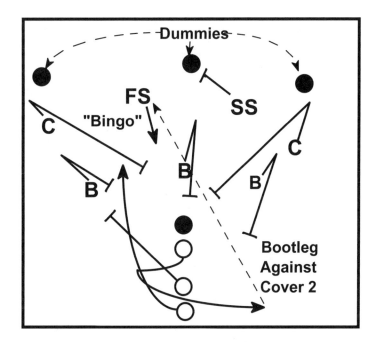

Figure 9–5 React and Score Drill

There are many other drills that can be devised and implemented to effectively train the young men who are chosen for this position. But we must remember that in the game of football, as in most all endeavors that we attempt, it's not just practice that makes perfect. It's *perfect* practice that attains the perfection for which we strive.

Part IX

Offensive Fundamentals of the Game

Chapter 10

Offensive Philosophy

Diversity

Offensive football *has* changed in the fifty-plus years that I've been in coaching. When I started coaching, offensive football was "hunker-down-and-fire-out" power football. When we reviewed the films on Saturday morning, there were twenty-two players within five yards on either side of the ball. Then along came the veer, and we were told that this offense allowed us to run the ball without blocking everyone on defense. The quarterback would handle two or three defenders with a read. Then innovative football minds began to "spread the field" with what they called the West Coast offense. The quarterback lined up in the backfield like the old single-wing attack of back in the early years of the sport. The difference was that now, instead of reading folks on the line, he and the receivers were reading defensive backs and reacting accordingly. When I go to ball games today, I can't help noticing that they don't block and tackle as they used to do. Today, many teams are running the zone-blocking scheme, and there's not much need to work on blocking. Eighty percent of the plays are passes, and those who *do* run the ball teach their linemen to latch on to a jersey and stay in front of the defender. Although most of my friends and many of my enemies still know me as "Off-Tackle John," I wasn't so stubborn (or stupid) that I didn't adjust to the times. I'm still a firm believer that coaches of the most successful programs are able to run some of all the above. As I watched the 2006 National Champions, the Florida Gators, I saw them run a multiple offense that included the spread-passing game, the zone-running game, and on the goal line and short yardage, the Single Wing and Stack I. This concept goes back to my discussion of studying the game and understanding all the aspects of various schemes. Other coaches tell me that I can't teach all these schemes as well as I could if I concentrated on one in particular. This might be true if I try to incorporate the entire package of every system. The trick is to devise a set of blocking rules and simple terminology that are adaptable to all *you* wish to include in *your* offensive package. Regardless of the offense you settle on, you must still remember that they don't give you points for *almost* scoring. When you get down to the ten-yard line, that zone you've been blocking has suddenly gotten full with the defensive backs lined up within five yards of the ball. When the entire defensive line is in a goal-line charge and the linebackers are touching the butts of the linemen, it's pretty hard to grab a little jersey and create a running lane. This is where that old "hunker-down-and-fire-out" power football is still very useful. This is just as true on the fifty-yard line when it's third and one and you must maintain possession to ensure the game. It's these crucial situations that win or lose ball games.

Offensive-Line Blocking Schemes

I previously mentioned the diversity of the offense of the 2006 National Champions— the Florida Gators. I've never won a national championship, but I've always tried to have as many offensive and defensive schemes as my teams could mentally absorb and physically execute. Through the years I also found that they can usually absorb much more that we give them credit for. It goes back to what I said earlier—with an adaptable set of rules and simple terminology both offensively and defensively, along with much repetition—the young, eager teenage minds can soak up just about anything we are willing and able to throw at them. In my career we have won many games and several championships, but the one honor that was especially rewarding to me and my coaching staff we received while coaching in Alabama. We were selected as the "Best-Prepared Team in Alabama" by a poll of coaches and sports writers. I discovered a long time ago that *success,* without *preparation,* is nothing more than *pure luck!*

Back to the copycat feature of winning coaches—if a multiple offense is good enough for the National Champion Gators, I figure it's good enough for John Meadows. The following pages contain terminology and drills that have been helpful in implementing our various offensive-blocking schemes:

1. Zone

2. Power blocking

3. X blocking

The Zone

In the late 1960s I attended a coaching clinic at the University of Alabama. One of the speakers at that clinic was John McKay, Head Coach at the University of Southern California. I still have the notes from that presentation when Coach McKay gave us the basics of Southern Cal's running game. Although he did not call it the Zone, the terminology and techniques he used were very similar to that used by coaches today that employ this popular offensive scheme. He spoke of "vertical splits" that are necessary to "read" and block a slanting defense. Over and over he used the expression "Running backs have eyes," meaning the ability to find and hit the seams created by what he called the "Overblock." He showed us films of O.J. Simpson and Mike Garrett getting the ball seven yards deep in the I-Formation and breaking the same play from one tackle to the other while the offensive line stepped into an "overblock," maintaining contact with defensive personnel who were in various defensive alignments. The following is a depiction of the play shown as McKay diagrammed it against a stunting 50 defense popular at the time:

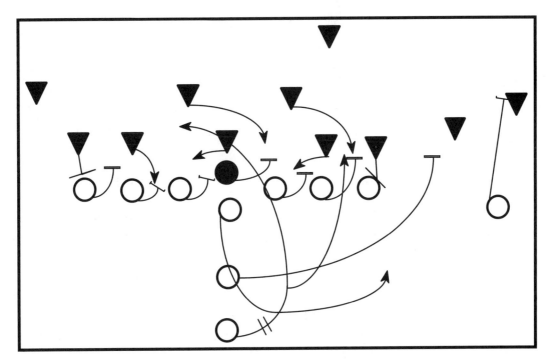

Figure 10–1 Overblock

ZONE BLOCKING: OFFENSIVE-LINE TECHNIQUES AND DRILLS

Following are the basic components of the modern-day zone-blocking scheme that is popular from the peewees to the pros:

STANCE

(**NOTE**: Some coaches who employ the Zone, especially in a spread offense, prefer offensive linemen to align in a "pass-set" stance for all plays (run or pass) to minimize predictability based on the offensive-line stance. Conversely, other coaches may prefer the traditional "hand-on-the-ground" three-point stance for run plays or for both run and pass plays.)

- Feet shoulder-width apart
- Flat back—eyes up
- "Z" in the knees

Figure 10–2 Stance

Three-point stance: (Some coaches prefer to have the playside hand down.)
- Approximately fifty-five to sixty percent of weight should be forward. (Linemen should be on the balls of their feet with heels slightly off the ground.)
- Off-hand should be positioned with open fist, just off the hip, with the thumbs up. (Many offensive linemen have a tendency to get in a three-point stance with their elbow resting on their thigh, often leading to uneven weight distribution and a critical delay in being in the "ready" position on their first step.)

ALIGNMENT

Proper vertical as well as horizontal splits are necessary and very advantageous in blocking the zone.

- Vertical splits (shown in Figure 10–4) can help negate a fast, penetrating, or stunt-heavy defense by providing the offensive lineman an extra step and additional space to read the defense, pick up stunts, and create blocking angles necessary to execute various blocking schemes.

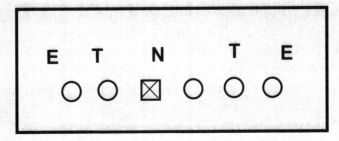

Figure 10–3 No Vertical Splits

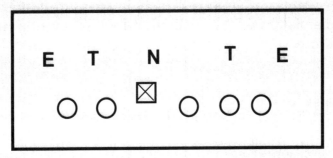

Figure 10–4 Good Vertical Splits

- Horizontal splits are used to widen or tighten defensive men "in the box." This creates wider running lanes for the inside-zone play or getting your ball carrier to the outside more quickly on the zone stretch.

FIRST STEP (CRITICAL!)

The importance of the first step cannot be overemphasized. Although zone blocking is a relatively simple concept, to execute it correctly and successfully, countless reps and much practice are needed to ensure that the offensive line comes off in unison and develops the ability to make decisions on the run.

- The first step is with the playside foot and is referred as a read step or bucket step.
- This read step is a short, six-inch step, gaining a little upfield ground.
- With this step, emphasize a solid base with their shoulders squared to the line of scrimmage. This eliminates seams that would allow the defense to penetrate, disrupting the play before it develops.
- Simultaneously with the first step, the offensive linemen's hands are brought to what many coaches refer to as the "drawn pistols" position, that is, hands cocked at the hips, open palms, thumbs up, and elbow in tight at approximately 90 degrees.
- This first step needs to be drilled with both feet with as many reps as are necessary to cause the appropriate action to become automatic. This is easily drilled as a rapid-fire, whole-group activity.
- Coaching points for this drill include eyes up, flat back, shoulders square, pistols drawn, knees bent, all while maintaining a good athletic position.

SECOND STEP

- This is a positioning step that is determined by the position of the defense on the snap of the ball and the particular point of attack, whether the inside zone or the zone stretch.
- When engaging down linemen or stunting linebackers, the offensive linemen should "shoot" their hands simultaneously with their second step.
- Coaching points for the second steps: elbows in tight, thumbs at twelve-o'clock, attack breastplate of defender, keep butt down, "block with your eyes", all while maintaining a good athletic position.

SUBSEQUENT STEPS—"POWER STEPS"

- Once the offensive lineman has engaged the defensive man, it is imperative that he does not get overextended.
- To ensure proper positioning, linemen must focus on taking "power steps"—short, choppy steps with feet at shoulder width. (I tell them to think of pushing a car out of a ditch.)
- Locking up and maintaining contact with the defender is much more important than attempting to "flat back" him. Offensive linemen must remember that "the backs have eyes" and that running with the defender allows the back to make appropriate cuts.
- These steps can be drilled using boards approximately 18 inches wide and 12 feet long using a dummy, a partner, or simply executing these steps "on air."

THE ZONE DRILL

Below is one of the simplest, most effective drills for both the offensive and defensive linemen for preparing to execute or defend the Zone:

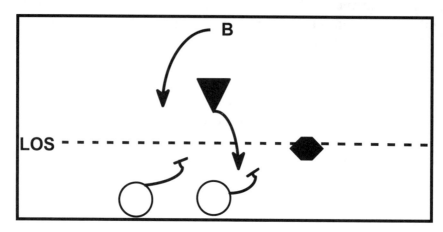

Figure 10–5 Zone Drill

The coach gives the DL the direction to slant. The LB scrapes the opposite.

The following diagrams show the basic Zone play with the various line calls we use to assure the best angle for our linemen:

ZONE READ RIGHT

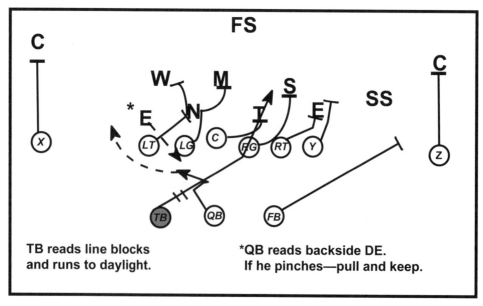

Figure 10–6 Zone Read Right

GAC CALL
(**G**uard **A**round **C**enter)

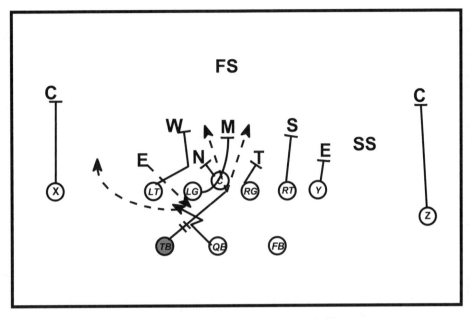

Figure 10–7 Guard Around Center

TAG CALL
(**T**ackle **A**round **G**uard)

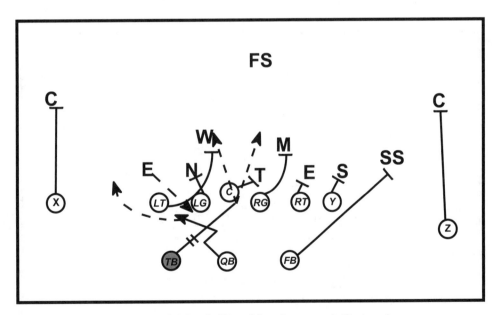

Figure 10–8 Tackle Around Guard

ACE CALL
(Double A-Gap Man)

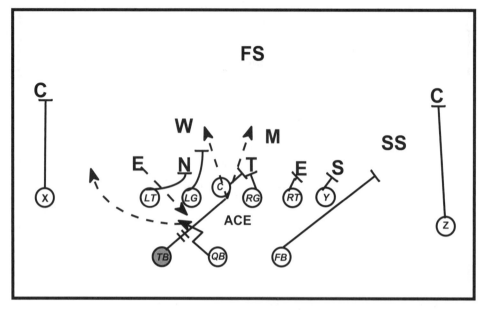

Figure 10–9 Double A-Gap Man

DEUCE CALL
(Double B-Gap Man)

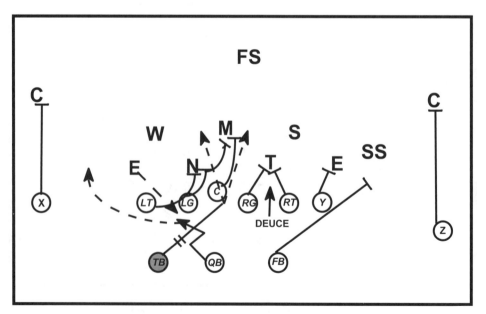

Figure 10–10 Double B-Gap Man

TRACE
(Double C-Gap Man)

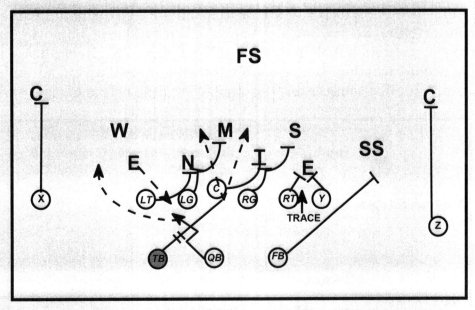

Figure 10-11 Double C-Gap Man

EAT
(End Around Tackle)

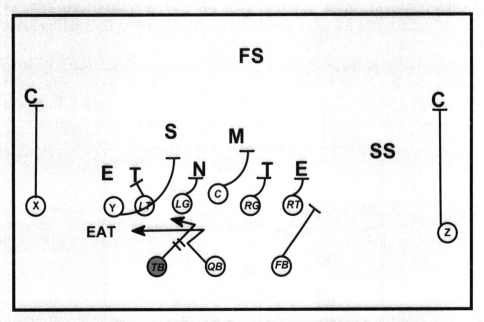

Figure 10-12 End Around Tackle

Power Blocking

A power-blocking scheme means that we are going to have a double-team block at the point of attack. I've always told our guys that if two of ours can't block one of theirs, we're going to get beaten. Our *two* must get movement on their *one* to create a bubble for our back's aiming point. Regardless of the point of attack, whether we are doubling the man lined up on our end, our tackle, our guard, or our center, the same technique is taught.

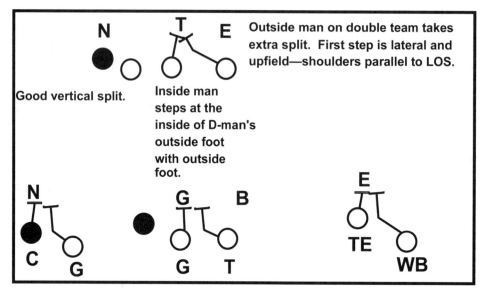

Figure 10–13 Double-Team Blocking

In each of the examples shown, if the defensive man disappears to the inside, the outside man will go to the next level, looking for linebackers. We tell him his rule becomes "backer—backer—safety." This means that if the man to be doubled disappears, he steps upfield, looking for the onside LB. If he is gone, he looks for backside linebacker. If he is gone or blocked, he plants his foot and runs laterally, looking for a defensive back filling over the top. We also tell him that this has to happen faster than we can say it!

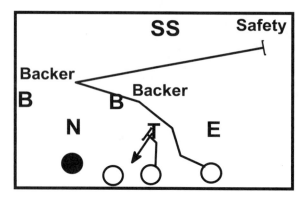

Figure 10–14 Backer-Backer-Safety

In some defensive alignments, a double-team block is not possible, but the bubble is created by their *alignment*. We say that they are *blocked by alignment*. The following example shows this rule against an eagle look on the strong side (Figure 10–15). In this alignment, expect the defensive end to line head-up with your tight end and squeeze the off-tackle hole. The tight end has the same alignment and lateral upfield step as he would if executing the double-team block. Although the tackle is blocked by alignment, the tight end's vertical split and first step will sometimes release him on the linebacker and isolate the defensive end for a kick-out block by either our back or the guard. If the defensive end runs a hard into the "C" gap, we tell the tight end that "nothing crosses your face" (Figure 10–16). This is the rule for any down blocker, and it tells him that he must lock up on the defensive man running the hard, stop his penetration, and use his momentum to carry him away from the play.

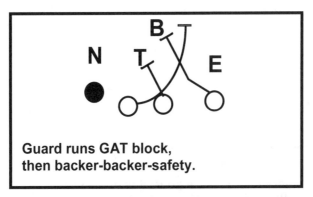

Figure 10–15 Blocked by Alignment

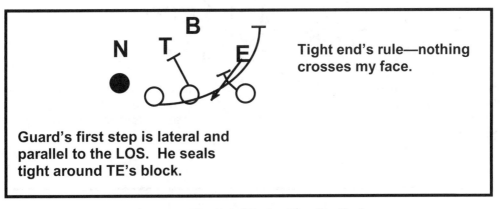

Figure 10–16 Tight End's Rule

X Blocking

Later I will elaborate on the attributes of the perfect offensive lineman—6'5"—300 pounds—and runs a 4.8 forty. Most of us won't have the luxury of coaching this gentleman very often. If we have five of these guys to line up over the football every Friday night, we wouldn't need many blocking rules or techniques. All we would need to tell them is what an old coaching friend of mine who, at one time, held the record for the most successive wins in the state. He humbly told me, "John, all I teach my linemen is how to hunker down and fire out—mostly how to fire out." Since I never had those five guys, I always had to teach our linemen how to read the defense and to make calls that would give them blocking angles and an advantage over a more physical player. I will give a simple illustration from what, admittedly, is one of my favorite plays—the lead play. One season we opened with a team in another state who was the eventual runner-up to the state champions on a field where they had a long winning streak of opening games. They played an even defense with different looks in the middle. With a second-string tailback, we ran the lead for the first thirteen plays, using the following blocking scheme: an X Block with a backside 2–3 call.

X BLOCK

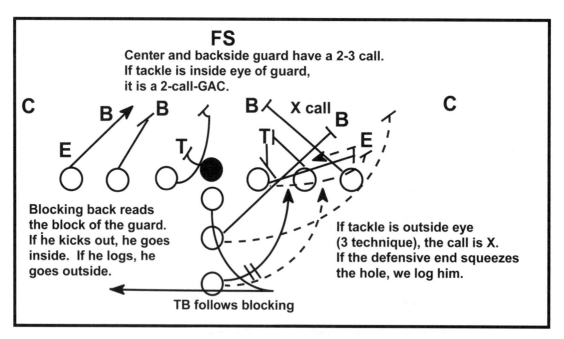

Figure 10–17 X Block

REGULAR BLOCK

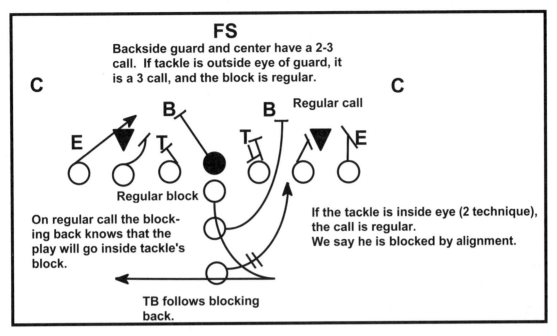

Figure 10–18 Regular Block

Blocking by Backs on Ends and Linebackers

I believe that anyone who knows anything about me or who has read any portion of this book knows that if you get ready to play me, you better prepare to stop the run. A high percentage of our offensive practice time is spent on developing and teaching blocking schemes and techniques that will produce seams in your defense that will allow our running backs to get at least our production goal on every play—four yards. I believe that of all the aspects of the game of football, the most unnatural and thus the most difficult to teach and to learn is that of blocking. If you think about it and break down all that is involved in playing the game, the natural attributes of running, throwing, catching, and tackling are those that we develop from the time we first learn to walk. On any playground in America, we see small kids running and trying to keep other kids from catching them. One of the first toys we throw into a baby's crib is a ball that we will toss to him, trying to develop his eye-hand coordination. Even playing defense is a natural reaction. If someone is pushing or holding us, trying to keep us from reaching a desired goal, the natural thing we do is push him aside to get to where we want to go. But, on the other hand, when we are asked to make contact with someone, and not to grab hold of him, but to make him go in a direction opposite the way he wants to go, that is very hard and unnatural and usually not first on the list of positions anyone would like to play. If I weigh 250 pounds and am proud of my sub-six forty time, I pretty much know that my jersey will come from the stack that has the numbers 50 through 79 stenciled on them. I have found that, for the most part, offensive linemen actually take pride in knowing that the only people who realize their importance are their coaches, the backs, each other, and, of course, their own mamas and daddies. This brings us to the topic of this section: "Blocking by the Backs." I've described the coaching techniques (that I have seldom had to use) that I've employed to teach the prima donna running back the value of his overweight teammates lined up in front of him. I have usually been blessed with young men who are team players and who realize the importance of contributing on every play—with or without the football. My philosophy for winning consistently has always been three times four equals twelve—move the chains. Keep that high-powered offense you're playing against on the sidelines sucking on Gatorade. Therefore, given the choice, I'll take that "blocking machine", who may be a step slower, over the "speed merchant", who wouldn't block his mama, every time. As a high school coach, one must realize that in the leagues below high school, from the peewees through junior high, those young men who may be a little more mature and blessed with speed are never taught to block—mainly because they are always running the ball. By the time they reach a good high school program, those other kids have caught up with them, and the defensive coordinators for your opponents can devise defenses that can contain that speed. Now we're back to where we started on that job description of the successful football coach—you've got a *selling job* to do on these fellows *before* you can begin your *teaching job*. The lucky coach has a super salesman on his side, and that is *depth*. When I have more than one or two adequate running backs, it doesn't take long for the non-blocker to realize that his stats will go up considerably when he joins up and improves his skills in this most important component of the game.

Although the papers they are written on have turned a pale yellow, the notes I scribbled down at a coaching clinic years ago are as valid today as when I took them. The heading at the top of the page reads "Blocking by the Backs," and although the speaker was introduced as the running-back coach from Penn State, he spoke for a good solid hour during this session on blocking. This coach equated the technique used to coach the backs to block with that of coaching the linebackers to play their position. "The only difference," he explained, "is that the linebackers are taught to grab hold and lock up with their opponent." The four things stressed for both positions were block or tackle with your eyes, sink your tail, run your feet, and keep an inside-out relationship. I did modify the terminology and adjusted other small details to better suit what we did, but the basic concept has never changed. Ninety percent of what we ask the back to do on any running play where he is designed to be in the blocking scheme is to lead through or to kick out. All coaches know the importance of "reading the blocks" by the guy who is carrying the ball. Just as important is to teach the blocking back the calls and schemes that we use with the offensive line to develop angles so that he too can read the defense even before the snap. The following examples are basic drills, coordinated with the offensive line, that we use for the blocking backs against an even front:

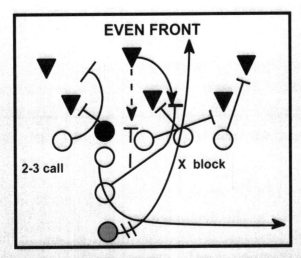

Figure 10–19 Even Front Drill

Above is the basic lead play against a 4–4 defense. On this play our primary read is the first defensive lineman head-up or outside the guard. On this look, to create angles, the strong-side linemen have an X block, and the backside guard and center have a 2–3 call. As our backs line up, they are listening for the call on the LOS as well as observing for themselves the defensive alignment. Both the fullback and the tailback know before the snap that our running lane is going to be outside the 3 Technique in the B gap. The fullback will take an inside route, aiming at the guard's butt and reading the playside linebacker. If the backer shoots inside, he seals him inside; otherwise, he continues on his inside-out route and either seals the backer or kicks him out.

After we drill against any possible stunt against the even-man line, we do the same thing against an odd front. On his odd front, the tackle gives a call that denotes whether the defender is head-up, inside, or outside. If the defender lines up inside or outside the tackle, he is blocked by alignment and pre-read by the backs.

112 BACK TO THE BASICS: WINNING IS MORE THAN X'S AND O'S

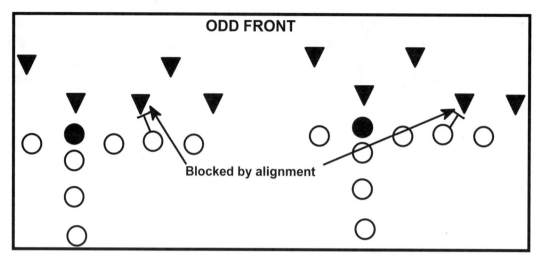

Figure 10–20 Odd Front Drill

If he lines head-up, both the tackle and the backs read his first move. We tell the tackle to step at the defensive tackle's outside foot with *his* outside foot and to read his first step. We expect him to pinch, and if he does, we use his momentum to wash him to the inside.

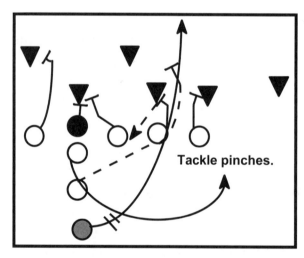

Figure 10–21 Tackle Pinches

As shown, if the tackle slants out, the play will be run inside.

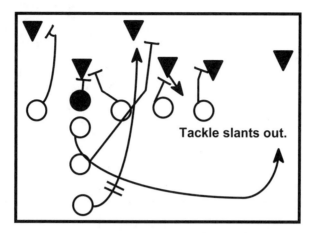

Figure 10-22 Tackle Slants Out

Besides the lead block on the linebacker, we also ask our backs to take on what are usually the second-best athletes on defense—the defensive ends. Blocking the linebackers usually involves taking on an aggressive, attacking-type defender while the defensive ends can be on a hard rush or standing tough with their "butt in the chute and their shoulders parallel." In either case we tell our guys that if they can establish a stalemate, they win. As with blocking the linebackers, our backs have a read on their first steps. To establish that good inside-out blocking angle we strive for, we tell our blocking back that for our off-tackle play, his aiming point is the inside butt cheek of the offensive tackle.

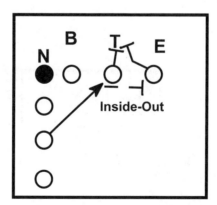

Figure 10-23 Defensive End Blocking

On his first read steps, he must recognize the technique of the defensive end. If the end is crashing, the back knows that he will have the same block that he has on the lead play with a pinching tackle—kick out or seal the linebacker.

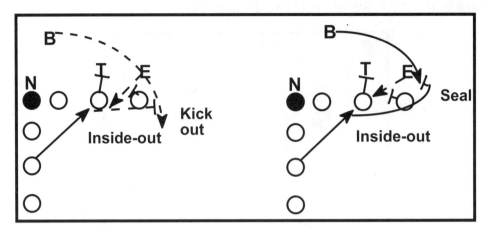

Figure 10–24 Kick-Out or Seal

If the defensive end is playing his read technique, he'll be on the LOS in a good football position, ready to take on the block of the back. He is told not to be reached or to be kicked out and to keep his outside arm free. If this is the read we get, for the play to be successful, the blocking back must execute the block, using all four of these essentials already described: block with your eyes, sink your tail, run your feet, and keep an inside-out relationship. Another key element for a successful power play is our premise that two of ours had better be able to block one of yours. This being the case, that stalemate established by the blocking back is all that is necessary for us to get our four yards. From seven yards deep the tailback has the same reads as the blocking back and linemen have, and he too must approach the LOS under control, with that inside-out relationship, hitting the bubble established by the double team.

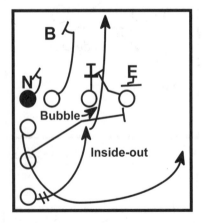

Figure 10–25 Hitting the Bubble

On the "end-pinch" read, the blocks of the fullback have been shown—kick out or seal the linebacker. Following the read of the fullback, the tailback will either hit the seam inside the block if the linebacker scrapes too wide or outside if the linebacker scrapes tight. We tell the tailback to get all the block he can and then get north and south—"Get me *my* four yards!" (Coaching point to the quarterback: Get the ball to the tailback as deeply as possible, giving him room to make his read.)

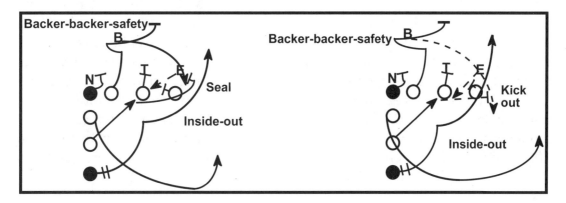

Figure 10–26 End-Pinch Read

I have shown just the basic drills and reads that we have for our basic power-running game—the lead and the power off-tackle. These drills will be modified, depending on the scouting report for the particular defense that we expect to see on Friday night. I assure you that you can't draw up a defense that I haven't seen or prepared for. One may look at these diagrams, read the coaching points that we stress, and think that time would not allow us to perfect the reads and schemes shown. Let me emphasize again that I was not called "Off-Tackle John" because I would *like* to be able to run the football between each C gap. I *was* going to run the football there, and everybody I played knew it. We worked on the *little things* involved in blocking: proper splits (horizontal and vertical), first step, reading the defensive alignment, and proper angles almost every day (without pads) in the off-season. *Repetition* is the key factor in doing anything well. That, plus a mindset that we try to instill in our players that (all things being equal) we can run at any defense you throw at us, earned me that nickname that I wear with pride.

Blocking by Wide Receivers

The primary attribute in this position is, of course, the ability to catch the football. With a good running game and the constant threat of a play-action pass, it becomes much easier to convince even the most stubborn, high-strung receiver that he is also an integral part of our ground game. On many of our running plays, if the defender locks up man, we tell the receiver to take a hard outside release and take him as deep as possible. When the defender recognizes run and leaves the receiver, he must find the football and try to get in the running lane. We tell the receiver to read the defender's feet. If he takes a drop step, that is the indication that he has determined run, and the receiver must reach an inside-out position, break down in a good football position, chopping his feet. If the defense is in Cover 3, the receiver must come off the LOS each play as if it is a pass play. He must make the defender play pass first since this will greatly facilitate his run blocking. The receiver's angle off the LOS will vary with his alignment. A playside receiver should realize that his corner will have secondary contain; therefore, the desired inside-out leverage needed to perform the block should be more easily attained. If the receiver lines up backside, he will have to take a more severe inside release to get the inside-out position in order to get between the defender and the football. A good receiver who is a team player and will go 100% on plays in which he is not getting the ball can turn a short gain into the game-winning touchdown.

Most Successful Plays

The successful coach always has at his disposal three or four short-yardage plays that will go against any defense anywhere on the field. On short yardage I like a balanced offensive set for basically two reasons: This keeps the defense balanced, and should they overload one side or if scouting reports indicate a weakness (or strength) in personnel, we can audible more easily. I particularly like the Stack I because this set allows a balanced power attack to either side.

The following plays (shown against a 6–5 goal-line defense) have been our most successful plays in short-yardage situations:

STACK I—POWER OFF-TACKLE

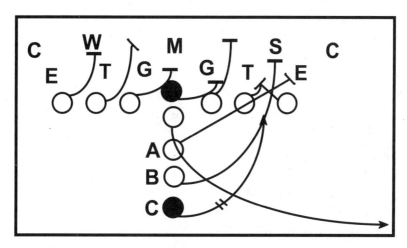

Figure 10–27 Stack I—Power Off-Tackle

Coaching Points: On the goal line we will tighten up the horizontal splits but will still take our normal vertical split to give us better angles on our scoop blocks and an extra half-step to read any stunts. We want a double-team block at the point of attack if at all possible.

Playside

Tight End—Take a four-foot horizontal split which will enable you to take a lateral read step at defensive tackle. The offensive tackle gives the tight end the alignment of the defensive tackle—head-up/inside/outside. If the defensive tackle is head-up, look for a slant inside, which puts you at the next level—tight off his butt. If he lines up inside, take your lateral step, keeping your shoulders parallel to LOS, and go to the next level. If he has an outside alignment, make contact, sink your tail to get movement, and create a bubble for our back to explode through. If defensive end is head-up, be alert for his pinching inside—"nothing crosses my face"—if he pinches, stop penetration and take him on down.

Tackle—Give tight end an alignment call—head-up/inside/outside. Head-up—take a read step at the inside of his outside foot with your outside foot. This, along with a good vertical split, will give you reaction time to his initial movement. If he slants inside, push hard off your outside foot and get your head in front of him, stopping his penetration but allowing his momentum to carry him away from the play. If he blasts or slants outside, stop his penetration with your eyes and an up-thrust with both hands under his shoulder pads. Sink your tail and coordinate movement with tight end to create bubble.

Guard—Step upfield with outside foot, staying low and bringing inside foot and shoulder through defensive guard, trying to get a piece of Mike linebacker. If you can make contact with Mike—keep contact and run your feet.

Center—Prior to the snap, shift your weight to backside foot so that at the snap you will be moving toward playside-gap player. Aim your backside shoulder at his outside knee and scramble your feet to stop penetration.

Backside G/T/E—Shoeshine (Chop playside gap.)

"A" Back—Aiming point is butt of offensive tackle "a hundred miles per hour." Make contact on the rise with first man who shows. Squeeze the hole—keep inside-out relationship.

"B" Back—Take short lateral step. Your aiming point is also butt of offensive tackle. Lateral step enables you to read "A" Back's block and to lead through the seam—or create one! If defensive end has pinched, expect to kick out linebacker who will scrape. Keep inside-out relationship.

"C" Back—Take short lateral step and aim for the butt of offensive tackle, reading block of "A" Back. We constantly remind him of the old coaching acronym: BYOB—Be Your Own Blocker. I also emphatically tell him, "This is *short yardage!* If it's third and three, you get *my* three before you try to add to *your* rushing stats!" Above all—PROTECT THE FOOTBALL!

Quarterback—Reverse out and ensure the hand-off. We insist on a convincing fake on *every* play. I tell him, "Although I called the play, I still want to think that *you* have the ball." I have seen a good fake "block" as many as three players on defense. If they don't honor the fake, we will run a keep or pass off this action.

I suppose that it was this play—or one like it—that is responsible for my nickname, "Off-Tackle John." Those who know me, and especially those who have played me, know that I *do* like to run the football, and I *will* establish a four-lane highway off a big tackle's butt if given half a chance. The years that I have had a big, blocking tight end to go with that big tackle, I have kept that other bunch's high-powered offense on the sidelines while I have run methodically up and down the field. As I stated earlier, the difference between *my* philosophy and that of many other coaches is that a four-yard gain for me is time for a celebration. I learned at an early age at Cedar Creek Elementary School that three times four is *twelve*, and it takes only *ten* to move the sticks. I have been known to repeat plays if they are successful, and I *do* consider a four-yard gain a success. When the outside veer first became popular, we put it in mainly because it *is* run off-tackle, and we *did* have two decent running backs and a running quarterback. That year, we played a team that had outstanding personnel but didn't have a clue on how to stop the outside veer. We ran fifty-seven offensive plays that night, and fifty-five of them were the outside veer. *They* never did stop us. We stopped ourselves a few times, or it could have gotten ugly.

The off-tackle power play has set up many other things for us through the years. One year, we did not have a kicker, not even a bad one. When we scored, we always went for two, figuring that we would make it at least fifty percent of the time. Our two-point play was always something coming off that power off-tackle play. We ran either a flood pass, a bootleg, or sometimes, depending on the defensive alignment, the power play itself. One Friday we traveled south to play one of the powerhouse teams in Montgomery. Their coach approached me before the game and made this declaration: "John, you may score on me tonight, but I guarantee you, you won't score off that two-point play you've run on everybody!" Bet! We took the opening kickoff, drove it the length of the field, and scored on (you guessed it)—Power Off-Tackle Right. Then we lined up in the same set and called the flood pass off the same play. Looking at the films the next day, we could see that they had really worked on stopping the flood. We snapped the ball, and our tight end, as he had been coached, butted the defensive end in the teeth as the end tried to grab him in a bear hug. When the quarterback rode the tailback at the off-tackle hole, it was too much for the poor fellow, and he let go of our end and mauled the faking tailback. Needless to say, our tight end was standing all by his lonesome in the corner of the end zone and caught the two-point conversion—just as planned! We scored one more touchdown that night and went for two as usual. But we fooled them again as we *ran* the ball at a defensive end who, after what I'm sure was a severe tongue-lashing after that first TD, was holding on to our tight end for dear life. We won the game 16–7, and the opposing coach had only four words to say to me as we shook hands at mid-field. In disgust, through gritted teeth, he spit out, "You did it again!"

STACK I DOUBLE LEAD

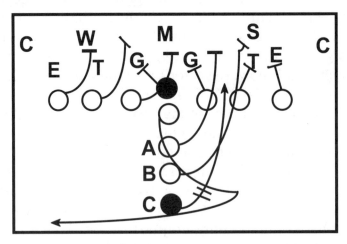

Figure 10–28 Stack I Double Lead

Coaching Points: Take normal vertical splits. Widen the horizontal splits 12–18 inches to create blocking angles and to widen the hole.

Playside

<u>Tight End</u>—Take three-foot horizontal split. If defensive end lines head-up, aim at his inside knee with your outside shoulder—*cannot* let defensive end pinch inside! If he slants outside, *do not follow him* but look for Sam and chop him (one inch above legal) if he blitzes.

<u>Tackle</u>—Read defensive tackle's alignment. If he lines up inside or outside, we say he is blocked by alignment. This makes for an easy read by the "B" Back. If he is head-up, take your read step—outside foot to inside of his outside foot. If he slants inside, get your head in front and drive him hard to create a hole. If he slants outside, get your head to the outside and turn him out. If he blasts, stop penetration and turn him in or out—butt to the hole.

<u>Guard</u>—If defensive guard is in the A gap, he is blocked by alignment. Explode your outside shoulder to his inside knee and do not allow any penetration.

<u>Center</u>—If backside defensive guard is head-up or in A gap, back block on him. Shift your weight to playside foot prior to snap. Aim playside shoulder at guard's backside knee, stopping any penetration.

<u>Backside Guard</u>—Give the center an alignment call for the defensive guard. If he is head-up or in A gap, gut block around center. Take one lateral

step toward play, close to the center's butt, keeping your shoulders parallel to LOS, no higher than your original stance. You are responsible for Mike should he blitz at "0."

Backside Tackle/Tight End— Shoeshine.

"A" Back—Aiming point, if defensive guard is in A gap, is offensive guard's butt. Squeeze the hole—maintain inside-out relationship. If Mike scrapes tight—seal him. If he scrapes wide, drive him out—maintain contact.

"B" Back—Pre-read defensive tackle's alignment. Inside or outside, he is blocked by alignment, and your path is determined accordingly. If he lines head-up, you must read the block of the tackle and react—inside or outside. Either way, you must maintain inside-out relationship, looking for Sam.

"C" Back—Take short lateral step, reading the defensive tackle. We want to run where he isn't. After your read (either by alignment or your tackle's butt), get all of the "B" Back's block you can with your head and shoulders turned upfield. Run smart—run hard!

Quarterback—Reverse out. Ensure the handoff. Turn and fake the bootleg.

The lead play may be the most frequently called play in football. You see it run at every level—from the neighborhood peewee team on Saturday morning to your favorite NFL team every Sunday afternoon. I always try to have a "hammer" in the backfield that had rather block than run the ball. One year I had a "*sledge* hammer," and we worked on this play against every conceivable defensive alignment every day. In fact, one day we had an hour-and-half scrimmage, and the only play we ran was some variation of the lead play. That same year we signed up a perennial powerhouse from the Atlanta, Georgia, area for our opening game. We had to play them on their home field that had a sign over the scoreboard in big red letters that declared this place to be "Death Valley." (I discovered very early in my coaching career that the more games you win, the harder it is to get a decent schedule.) We were told that this team had not lost an opening game in several years. That was soon to change. On the Monday before the game, we received the news that our 210-pound senior tailback lived in our city rival's school zone and was thus declared ineligible. We worked a smaller, slower junior there for three days, and with him—butterflies and all—sitting next to me on the bus on Friday morning, we rolled out of the parking lot headed toward Death Valley. Even with the loss of our starting tailback, our game plan didn't change. We were a power football team *with* him, and we were a power football team *without* him—just a little slower. The tone of the game was established on our first drive. They kicked the ball through the end zone, and we got it on the twenty. The first play we ran was the lead play over right tackle for eight yards. I'm sure that the old adage "If it ain't broke, don't fix it!" is no truer anywhere than in the game of football. Thirteen lead plays and an extra point later, the score was Home 0—Visitors 7. In that drive, we faced four different looks on defense, none of which either confused us or slowed us down. Needless to say, as well as we ran the football that night, our play-action passes looked as if our receivers were out to practice early. We ended that win streak of opening-game victories 27 to 14, and our second-team tailback ended up with 198 rushing yards, nearly all of which were behind the "Ole Sledgehammer" on the basic lead play.

STACK I FULLBACK WEDGE

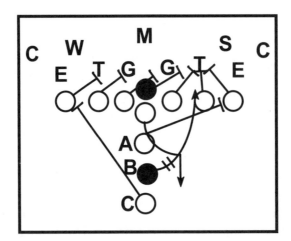

Figure 10–29 Stack I Fullback Wedge

Coaching Points: Tighten horizontal splits to 12 inches. This is a very short-yardage play, and we will run it behind our best blocker at whichever player the scouting reports tell us is the weakest.

<u>Playside G/T/E</u>—With the tackle as the apex, these three players come off the ball with their shoulders parallel with LOS and touching, forming a wedge or triple team on defensive player head-up or inside offensive tackle.

<u>Center and Backside Linemen</u>—Seal the near playside gap with shoeshine.

<u>"A" Back</u>—Seal tight off the butt of playside tackle (Inside-out).

<u>"C" Back</u>—Seal tight off the butt of backside tackle (Inside-out).

"B" Back—Run at the offensive tackle's butt, look for seam either right or left—lower shoulders—BYOB. Second and third efforts are often required to get the necessary yardage.

Quarterback—Ensure handoff! Drop straight back, grab passing hand with your other hand, and show pass. (Don't think that I won't slip one of the backs or ends out on fourth and inches from time to time!)

There's the time we were playing in a close and very heated contest with an archrival when, near the end of the game, we were trailing by five points on about the forty-five yard line. We were going in, and it was fourth and the length of the football. I called the wedge play and added, "Tight end—get lost." This was our pass off the fake wedge. We came to the line in our short-yardage package, and on the first sound, the line fired off, and our fullback hit the pile of humanity full speed. Our quarterback pulled the ball out, laid it on his hip, walked nonchalantly about five yards deep, and threw a perfect spiral to our tight end who was strolling naked down around the ten-yard line. He hauled it in and pranced into the end zone with what *should* have been the winning touchdown. Meanwhile, back at the line of scrimmage, the official was blasting on his whistle and searching in the pileup for the football. Inadvertent whistle! No touchdown! Now I'm usually not one to complain about the officiating, but the game *was* at their place, and the caldron of stew boiling in each end zone *did* make me a little suspicious.

DOUBLE-SCREEN READ

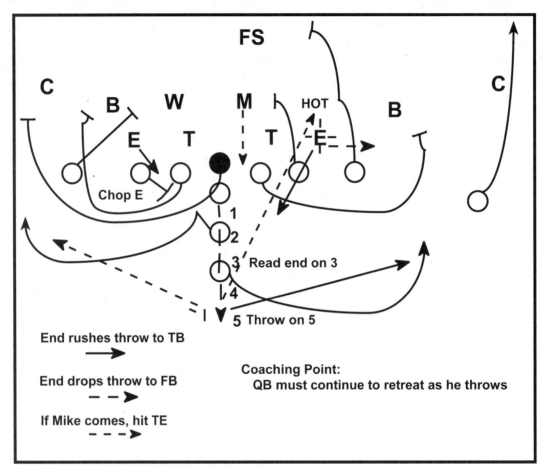

Figure 10–30 Double-Screen Read

Passing Package

Those coaches who know me and have given me the very appropriate nickname "Off-Tackle John" will do a double take when they see a section in my book with the heading "Passing Package." I will admit that when I look back to the game plans of my earlier years and the post-game stats, I can find those of one year when we were undefeated and averaged throwing only six passes per game. Many coaches adhere to the philosophy that if times and "football fads" change—*they* change. I prefer to remain staunch to the old cliché: "If it ain't broke, don't fix it." When the times and fads changed, I didn't change—I just adjusted and modified. I never did sell out to the schemes of pass first, run second. I look at the teams that win championships at every level and observe what they noticeably have in common—they play good defense and they *can run the football*. Of course those teams that carry home trophies complement these two winning attributes with a sound and simple passing game.

As I have mentioned earlier, I discovered at a very early stage in my coaching career that the hardest thing to coach in the game of football is blocking. To build on that assertion, I'll say that the hardest block to perfect is to protect the quarterback who is dropping straight back five to seven yards with what we term "cup protection." Good defensive coordinators came up with game plans that involved complicated stunt packages with the defensive linemen perfecting all sorts of techniques to get to that stationary target standing seven yards behind the line of scrimmage. With all of that said, it seemed obvious to me that I didn't want the one player whom I had coached the most standing there with a big bull's eye on his chest, waiting to take a ride off the field on the "Gator." In this section dedicated to what I term my "Passing Package," I'll show the protection and a few basic patterns that were successful for me through the years. I taught and had the most success with the following four types of passes, all of which employed very simple rules and easily executed protection: bootleg pass, screen pass, play-action pass, and three-step drop pass.

After I established a running game (which with me was usually done by reputation), I had several passes that came off each of my most successful running plays. The pass patterns would change, depending on the other team's defensive alignment and the scouting report. Yet the protection was always the same—sound and simple. The three types of protection that I employed off these running plays—bootleg, screen, and strict play-action—are shown on the next pages.

Bootleg-Pass Protection

The first example is our Bootleg Protection shown coming off our counter-trap play:

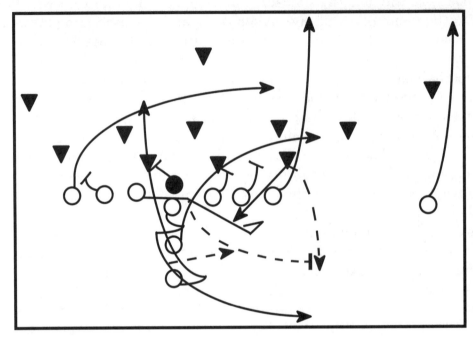

Figure 10–31 Counter Bootleg

Counter Bootleg

<u>Pulling Guard</u>—Take two flat steps, missing QB. Look to DE—read rush. If he shoots inside, adjust pull to block him with inside shoulder, sealing him inside. If he shoots upfield to contain, keep him outside.

<u>Center</u>—If uncovered, fill for pulling guard. If covered, along with backside guard, run a "standing overblock," blocking any middle stunt (Figure 10–32).

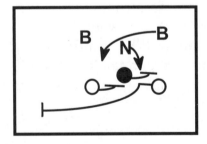

Figure 10–32 Standing Overblock

Backside Guard—If covered, block man on. If odd-man line, run a "standing overblock" with the center, looking for stunt (Figure 10–32).

Playside Tackle—Aggressively block man on if covered. Step at the inside of his outside foot with your outside foot—don't get overextended to the outside. If uncovered, protect the C gap.

Backside Tackle—First step is to inside. If covered, block man on; if not covered, hinge and block first thing that shows from backside.

Tailback—Counter step, show pocket, and read backside rush. If only one defensive man comes, carry out fake; if two come—*forget fake*—block number two (Figure 10–33).

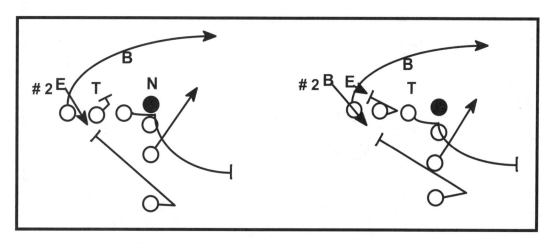

Figure 10–33 Read Backside Rush

Fullback—Find opening in either A or B gap—run route to flats.

Backside TE—Run drag route—adjust according to position of linebackers.

Playside TE—Run seam route between corner and safety.

Wide Receiver—Take off.

Quarterback—Reverse out—wave the ball at the FB and make decent fake to TB. Snap head quickly and find defensive end. If he is on a flat rush—you get depth. If he boxes to contain—set up and read pattern. Look deep first. If nothing's there, read playside linebacker.

Screen-Pass Blocking Rules

With the high school and college rules, which allow linemen downfield if the pass is thrown behind the line of scrimmage, I'm convinced that high school coaches do not take advantage of this often enough. Below I have inserted our **Screen Pass** coming off the counter trap and counter bootleg. Our screen rules remain the same regardless of the play or situation we use to set it up.

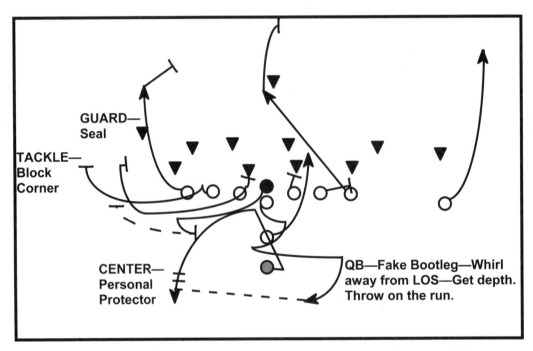

Figure 10-34 Fake Counter Bootleg Screen to TB

<u>Tailback</u>—Same rules as bootleg. After fake (or contact with #2), set up five yards deep outside tackle—position yourself in a clear line to QB.

<u>Center</u>—Stop quick penetration—set up between QB and TB. Block anyone who sees the screen and turns toward TB—ensure catch—if nothing shows, turn and lead play.

<u>Playside Tackle</u>—Stop quick penetration—get wider than outside man—kick or seal.

<u>Playside Guard</u>—Stop any quick penetration—get outside end and seal LB.

<u>Playside TE</u>—Push corner—block safety.

<u>Backside Guard/Tackle</u>—Block #1 and #2 on LOS.

Backside TE—Push through safety—block backside corner.

Wide Receiver—Push corner deep and outside.

COUNTER-BOOTLEG READ

I have had much success with this counter-trap series. After we master the trap, bootleg, and bootleg screen, we put in the counter-bootleg read shown below:

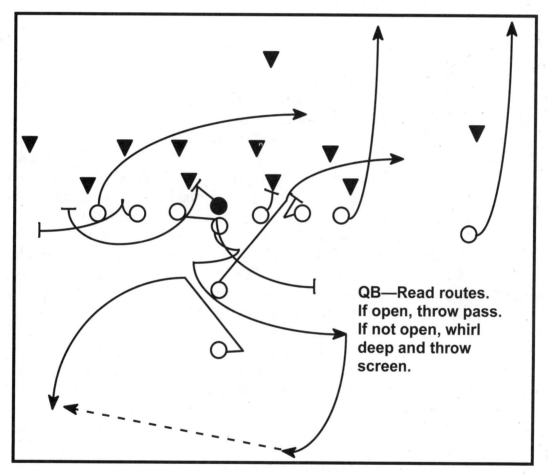

Figure 10-35 Counter Bootleg Read

All Receivers—Run counter-bootleg routes.

Tailback—Same rule as bootleg screen.

Playside Tackle—Same rule as counter bootleg.

Playside Guard—Same rule as counter bootleg.

Center—Same rule as counter bootleg—except after contact with defensive man, he becomes seal man on screen if QB's read dictates screen.

Backside Guard—Same rule as counter bootleg.

Quarterback—Same rule as counter bootleg—except if none of the routes are open, the play becomes the counter-bootleg screen and those rules apply.

Play-Action Pass Protection

During football season we constantly hear TV sports announcers admonish the coaches on the field to "establish the run" so that they can run play-action passes. As I have mentioned, when I stepped on the field, the run was already established—and so was my passing game. When he was the head coach at the University of Southern California, John McKay spoke at a football clinic that I attended at the University of Alabama. His topic was "The Passing Game at Southern Cal." This was during the era of great tailbacks at that school, and handing the ball to one of these All-American running backs lined up seven yards deep and having him run to daylight was their primary offense. It didn't take me very long into Coach McKay's presentation to decide that our playbooks must have rolled off the same printing press. His primary passing game was also play action. During his speech, he made this declaration: "If it's third and fifteen, we'll line up and run a play-action pass. I know that right now some of you are out there thinking: 'On third and fifteen, you're not going to fool anybody. Why would you run a play-action pass?'" His explanation confirmed what I had decided years earlier: "First of all, play-action pass protection is the safest and the simplest type of protection I can use. I don't care what the down and distance are—all you have to do is just wiggle the ball in the direction of O.J., and there's not a linebacker in America who won't hesitate for just a moment before he drops to his hook zone!" I never lined up O.J., but every coach I played knew that whoever dotted that "I" in my backfield was not going to have a problem getting to sleep that night after the game. The following diagrams show our basic play-action pass protection:

VERSUS 4-4

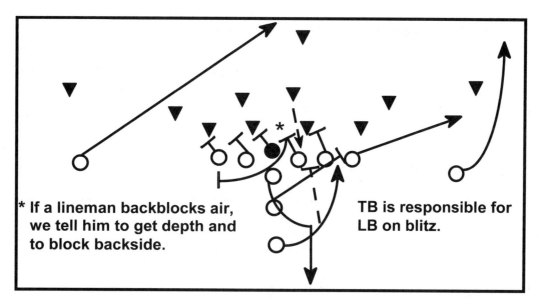

Figure 10-36 Versus 4-4

<u>Playside Tackle</u>—Aggressively block first man head-up or outside guard and inside defensive end.

<u>All Other Linemen</u>—Gap away. *Exception: If nothing shows in their gap, (right guard in diagram), we tell them to get depth and to check backside lanes.

<u>Fullback</u>— Run tight off tackle's butt—block first thing that shows.

<u>Tailback</u>—Run hard at playside linebacker—pick up any blitz.

<u>Quarterback</u>—Reverse out—fake off-tackle play. Read #2—if he comes, look for "hot route" (Figure 10-37).

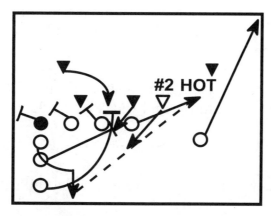

Figure 10-37 "Hot Route"

Sprint-Out Pass Protection

We worked our quarterbacks a lot on throwing on the run basically for the following simple and valid reasons: We felt that the protection was sound, and if he could run, this put more pressure on the defense. Also, when he turned upfield, with his added momentum, he could get more velocity on the ball. The following diagrams show our sprint protection with some of our basic routes and reads:

SPRINT PROTECTION

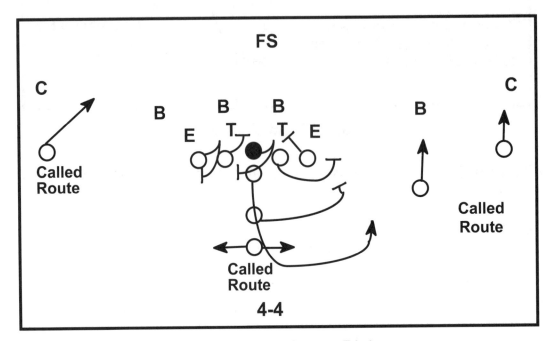

Figure 10–38 Sprint Right

<u>Right Tackle</u>—Block first down lineman head-up or outside the guard.

<u>Right Guard</u>—Pull and get depth—squaring shoulders to LOS—log the defensive end, sealing him inside. If defensive end boxes—seal him outside with help from fullback.

<u>Center</u>—Over and back—This term means that he will check the playside gap, and if nothing shows, hinge and check backside lanes.

<u>Left Guard</u>—Follow same rule as center.

<u>Left Tackle</u>—Follow same rule as center and left guard.

Fullback—Sprint hard playside parallel with LOS until you are outside defensive end—help seal.

Quarterback—Push off backside foot, bringing ball to throwing position. Get depth, sprinting through position where TB lined up. Read defensive end. If he is sealed inside, sprint to corner, turn shoulders to LOS—read route—throw off front foot. If defensive end boxes, set up and read route, throwing as if it is a drop-back pass (Figure 10–39).

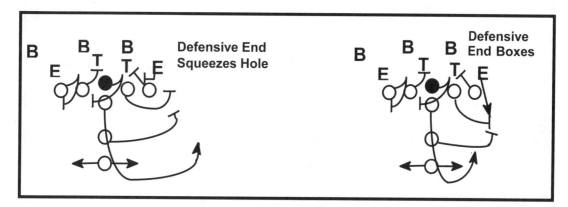

Figure 10–39 Defensive End Squeezes Hole or Boxes

*Coaching point: Coaches are alerted to this technique and will run the X Lead against a boxing end (Figure 10–40).

X LEAD

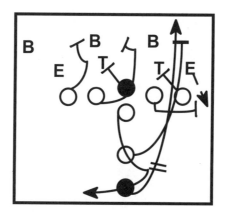

Figure 10–40 X Lead Against Boxing End

If all receivers are covered on the front side, the quarterback reverses field and looks for the backside receiver who is running what I call a scramble-out route (Figure 10–41).

SCRAMBLE-OUT ROUTE

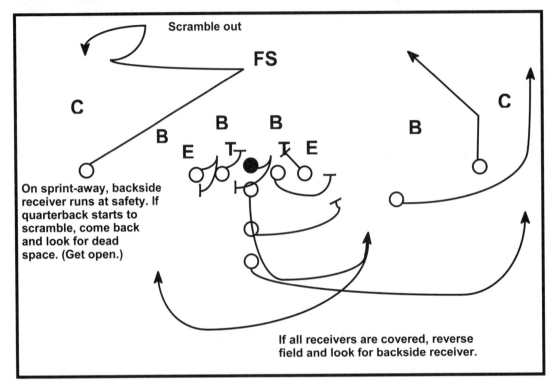

Figure 10–41 Scramble-Out Route

SPRINT-RIGHT WHEEL ROUTE

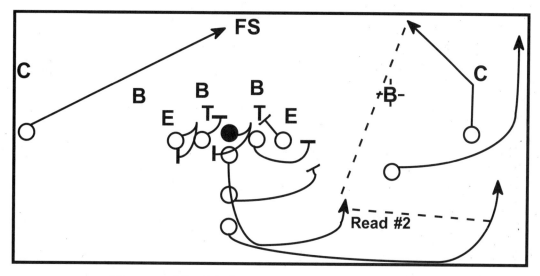

Figure 10-42 Sprint-Right Wheel Route

<u>Linemen/Fullback</u>—Sprint protection.

<u>Tailback</u>—Run swing.

<u>Quarterback</u>—Push off backside foot—seat ball—be ready to throw on third step. Read defensive end—get depth and sprint or set up and throw.

SPRINT-RIGHT WHEEL COMEBACK

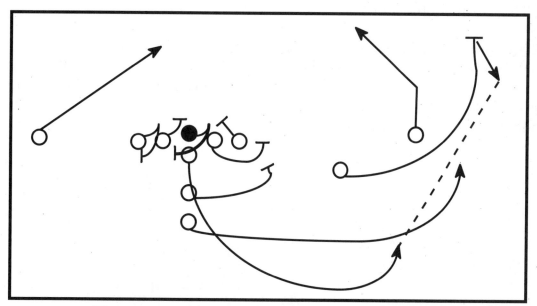

Figure 10-43 Sprint-Right Wheel Comeback

SPRINT-RIGHT SLANT OUT/READ

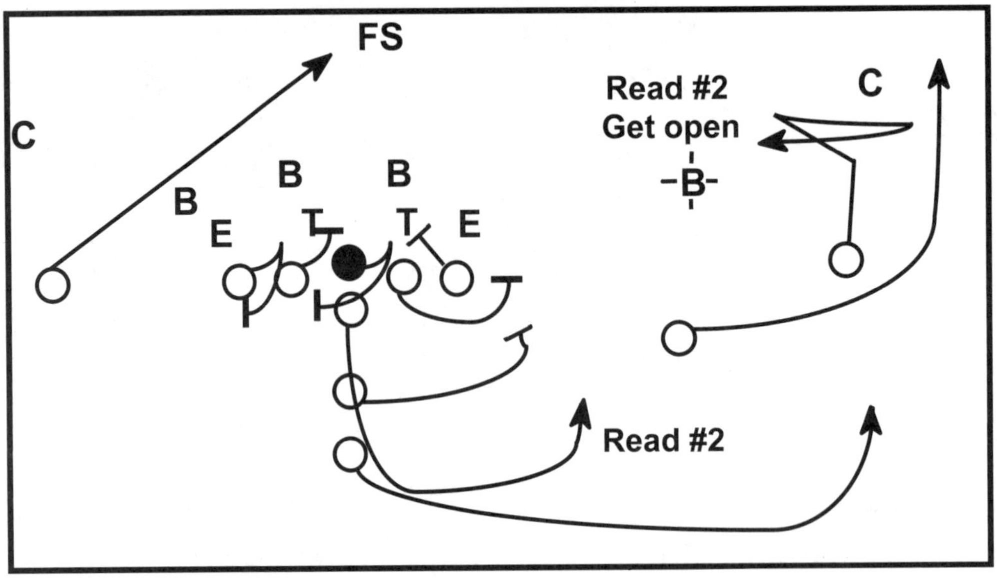

Figure 10-44 Sprint-Right Slant Out/Read

Three-Step Drop Pass Protection

The three-step drop pass is strictly a timing pass in which both the quarterback and the receivers read the coverage and react accordingly. Although we developed an entire package off this series, I'll show only a few patterns along with the easily taught protection. In this package, as mentioned, we taught the quarterback and the receivers to first pre-read the coverage upon alignment and then to read individual defenders as the play developed. First, I'll show the protection:

<u>Linemen</u>—Tighten horizontal splits and aggressively block the gap to your left. We tell them on this protection to block "low, hard, and mean." We want to make sure that we get the defensive linemen's hands down. **Coaching point: Do not** chase a defender who may line up in the left gap and stunt out of it—**protect your gap**.

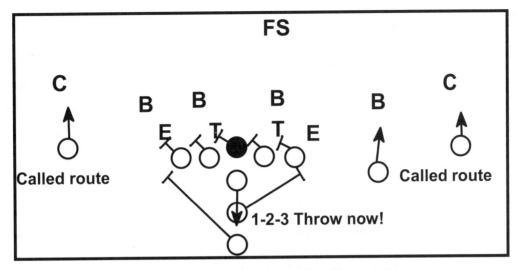

Figure 10-45 Three-Step Protection

- Exception: If defense lines up in a 50, the right tackle blocks man on unless linebacker is on the LOS in which case he still protects inside gap. Although this leaves defensive end free, we can still get the pass off if we throw on time—1–2–3 Throw now! (Figure 10–46).

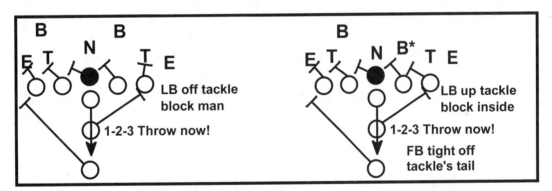

Figure 10-46 Three-Step Protection for 50

<u>Fullback</u>—Block right tackle's butt—block anything that shows "one inch above legal."

<u>Tailback</u>—Block left tackle's butt—block anything that shows "one inch above legal." (If nothing shows, we can use him as an outlet.)

Three-Step Drop Passing Package

In a book designed to stimulate only a thought process concerning various defensive and offensive schemes, it is impossible to include every coaching point and technique used in developing and perfecting each package. The following diagrams are very basic and certainly not comprehensive, but these are some very successful passes employed in the three-step drop series:

PASS 1

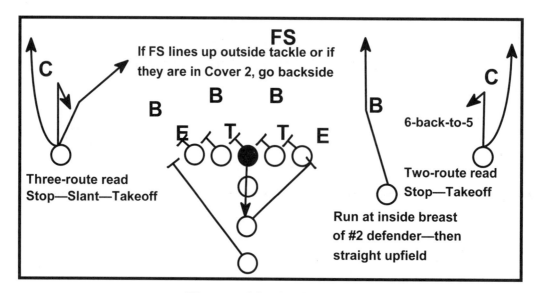

Figure 10–47 Pass 1

QB pre-reads defense:
- If only two defenders are outside the tackle box:
  - Throw to either side.
- If there are three defenders outside the tackle box:
  - Go to the single receiver side.

On the two receiver side:
- If two are in the box:
  - Read the corner.
- The receiver runs hard at the corner—every time!

If the corner stands and plays the stop:
- Throw takeoff.

If he backs up:
- Throw the 6-back-to-5 stop.

PASS 2

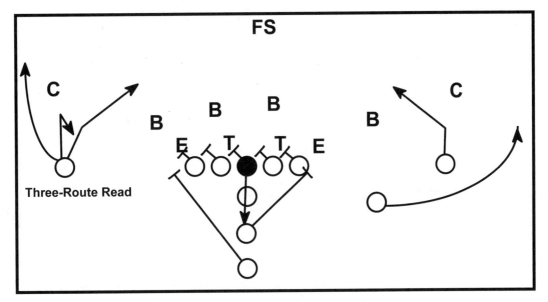

Figure 10-48 Pass 2

- Outside receiver runs slant
- Inside receiver runs wheel
- Read #2 defender.
- If they line up in Cover 2—Go backside.

PASS 3

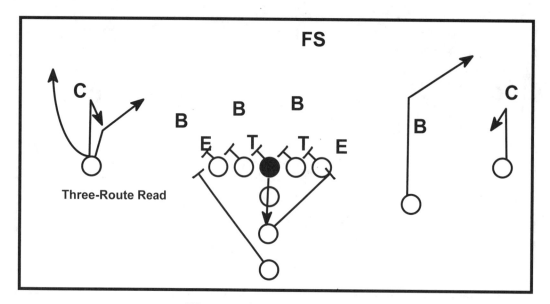

Figure 10–49 Cover 3

On Cover 3:
- Outside receiver runs a stop
- Inside receiver runs a post corner
- QB reads corner.

PASS 3

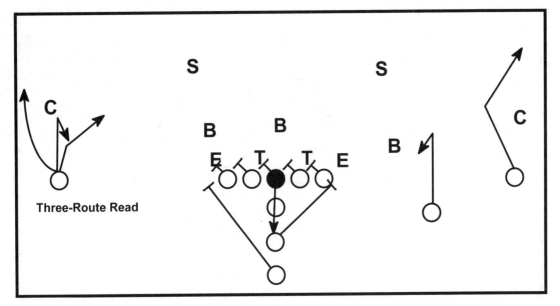

Figure 10–50 Cover 2

If they're in Cover 2:
- Inside receiver runs a stop.
- Outside receiver runs a post corner.
- QB knows that single receiver is running his three-route read.

PASS 4

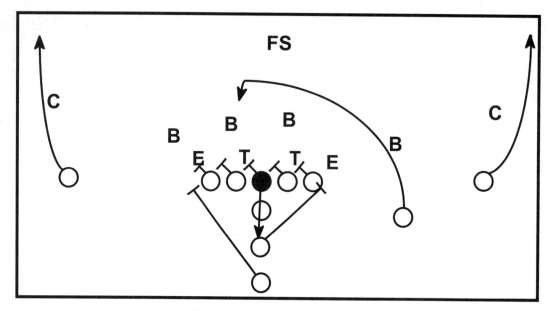

Figure 10–51 Pass 4

- Outside receivers run fades.
- Slot receiver spots behind LBs in front of safety.
- On Cover 2, QB must hit receiver in dead space between corner and safety.
- QB should decide which side he is going to before snap.
  Look to other side to move safety.

PASS 5

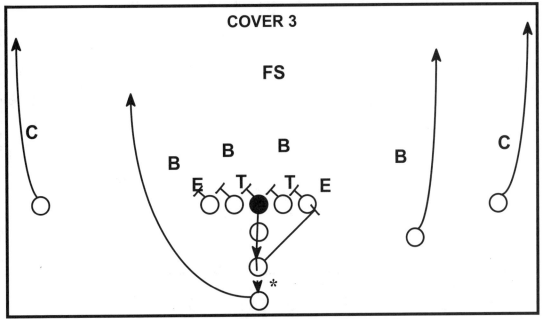

Figure 10-52 Pass 5 – Cover 3

All receivers (including tailback) run takeoffs.
QB's read is FS—He can move safety with eyes—Throw opposite.
*On this pass the QB takes a quick 5-step drop—Protection is the same.

On Cover 2 the inside receivers run takeoffs. Outside receivers run a 14-yard drift.

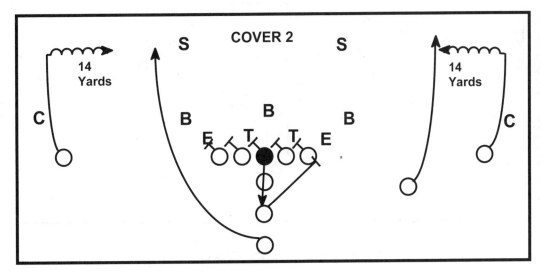

Figure 10-53 Cover 2

PASS 6

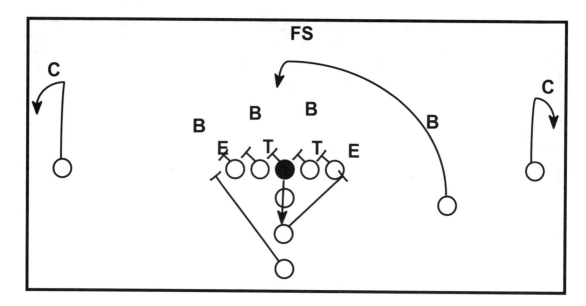

Figure 10–54 Pass 6

Outside receivers run a 6-back-to-5 out, which should be a bend out, NOT a ninety-degree angle. Slot receiver runs a spot route behind LBs in front of safety.

PASS 7

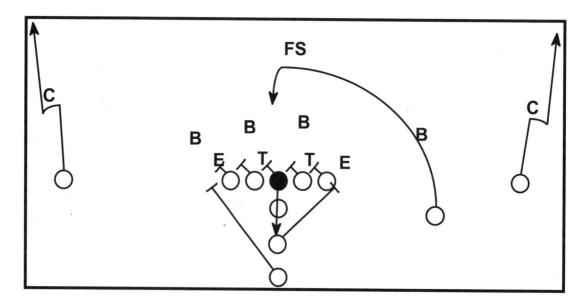

Figure 10–55 Pass 7

Outside receivers run a quick out-and-up. The slot receiver runs spot route behind LBs and in front of safety.

SPECIAL PLAYS

STACK I COUNTER TRAP

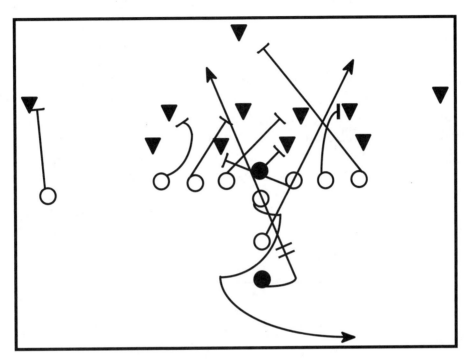

Figure 10-56 Stack I Counter Trap

Coaching Points: Trap the first man right or left of center. (Shown is an odd trap, using our terminology.) Our trap rule: first man head-up or outside the guard. We always call two plays in the huddle and let the QB audible at the LOS to the desired play for the defensive look. Although we prefer to trap the B gap and beyond, if a defensive man jitterbugs to the playside A gap—too late to audible—the guard knows to run an influence step and scrape the offensive tackle's tail. The tackle knows that it becomes a "swap" block, and he goes tight off A-gap player's tail and blocks backside LB (Figure 10–57).

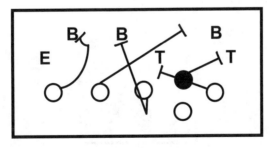

Figure 10-57 Swap Block

As shown, we always take good vertical splits. We tell the linemen to take *"appropriate"* horizontal splits; that is, a quick-trapping guard can take a wider split than a slower one can. Vertical splits will allow better blocking angles for the linemen who have backside down blocks.

Playside Guard—Take a *"common sense"* split—not so wide that it changes the defensive technique but as much as possible to create a wider running lane. Do not "wait" for a LB if it appears he is going to stunt. If LB stunts late, distance created by guard's vertical split should allow him to block his assignment—first man head-up or backside of center. If LB is on the LOS, the rule is same for all linemen blocking down—"nothing crosses my face." If backside LB disappears, the rule is always the same for all linemen who have LB responsibility—Backer-Backer-Safety (Figure 10–58).

Center—Uncovered—block backside, filling for trapping guard. Same rule as trapping guard—*do not* follow a down lineman outside—expect to block stunting LB (Figure 10–58).

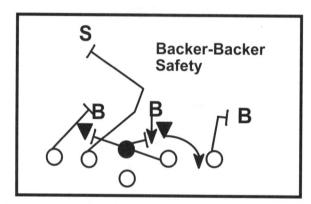

Figure 10–58 Backer-Backer Safety for Trap

If center is covered, he blocks through backside shoulder of nose to LB—carrying nose with him if he slants—in which case playside guard reads stunt and blocks backside LB (Figure 10–59).

Figure 10–59 Blocking X Stunt – Center Covered

Trapping Guard—Pull through the center's rib cage. **Do not** follow a down-lineman to the outside. If this happens, expect to block a stunting LB (Figure 10–60).

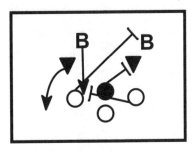

Figure 10–60 Trapping Stunting Linebacker

We tell the trapping guard to block whoever is there in the "ear hole" to prevent his falling into the running lane.

Playside Tackle—Block nearest onside LB except on "swap" block. If the defense jitterbugs to A gap (before QB can audible to desired play), the guard will (in a voice audible only to the tackle) repeat the change, "Swap, swap, swap," and the tackle will block the inside LB as shown in Figure 10–57.

Playside End—Release your *outside* shoulder through DE's *inside* shoulder. (Nothing crosses my face.) If DE pinches—cut him.

Backside End—Release inside of DE and get in running lane.

Wide Receiver—Push/block corner.

Fullback—Good fake into B gap. Seal pulling guard's tail—no penetration.

Tailback—Counter step away from call—throw hands and head—run straight at center's tail—read tackle's block on LB.

Quarterback—Reverse out—get off mid-line—quick fake to FB—look football into TB's pocket—turn and make good fake on bootleg.

STACK I QUARTERBACK SUICIDE

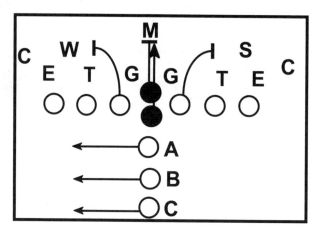

Figure 10–61 Quarterback Suicide

Coaching Points: You may look at this play and say to yourself, "He doesn't run that!" But he does! We take 18-inch splits with our guards and up to two feet with tackles and ends. Only three linemen move on this play.

<u>Center</u>—Snap the ball and make eye and hand contact with Mike linebacker. Try to turn your tail one way or the other. If you have a stalemate—you win!

<u>Both Guards</u>—Come off the ball with your outside foot and block Willie and Sam linebackers with inside shoulders.

<u>Quarterback</u>—Ensure the snap—tuck the ball and hesitate one-half count—follow the center. If Mike has stepped one way, you go the other. If there is a stalemate, choose a side and explode upfield.

<u>Rest of Backs</u>—Sprint left.

<u>Rest of Linemen</u>—Do not move!

I have scored on this play on more than one occasion. If it does nothing else, it will slow down the penetration in the A gap or at least make for an easier scoop by the guards and center. When I first put this play in many years ago, one of my assistants who had played for the legendary coach of the Chattanooga Moccasins, Scrappy Moore, recognized it and told this story: Chattanooga was a Division I AA school that always played three or four of the "big boys" every year, mainly for the revenue that these teams would pay to have a worthy breather inserted into their tough schedule. When Bear Bryant came to Alabama, Scrappy was on their schedule, but the Bear dropped him and gave as the reason, "We don't want to have to prepare that much for what's supposed to be a breather!" This assistant said that they put this particular play in during the walk-through on Friday afternoon before playing a big SEC school the next day. This last-minute insertion of this short-yardage play was a mystery until it was discovered that this SEC school was playing a conference rival the next weekend and that *they* ran this play. It seems that the coach of the team that Chattanooga was playing had called Scrappy and asked him to run it so that they could show it to their players on a game film. According to my assistant, the Mocs didn't have quite the success with the Quarterback Suicide that particular Saturday afternoon that I have had through the years.

REVERSE

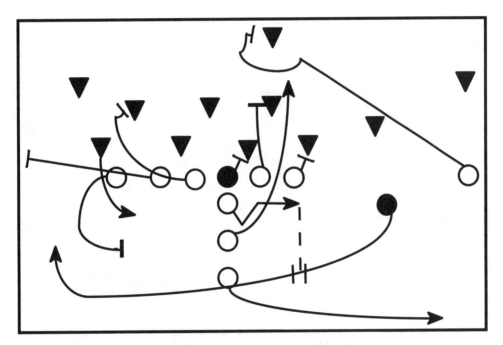

Figure 10–62 Reverse

Coaching Points: The basic rules for any reverse are the same: the outside man does a "whirl block," releasing inside defensive end, setting up between him and ball carrier. Wait until he turns—***don't clip!*** These diagrams show this block on three different sets. Depending on your set, this could be the tight end (Figure 10–62), tackle (Figure 10–63), or wingback (Figure 10–64). The next man kicks or seals the corner force. The third man from the end of line releases upfield and sets up between outside LB and ball carrier.

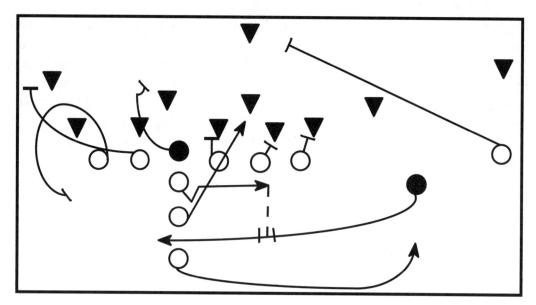

Figure 10–63 Reverse – Unbalanced Line

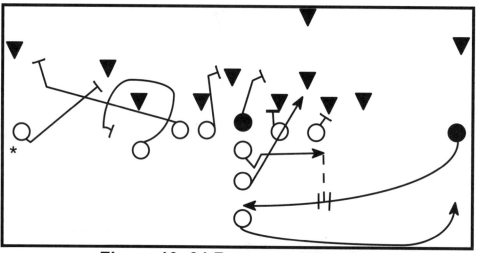

Figure 10–64 Reverse – Wing Set

* If there is a wide receiver outside the end man on the LOS, he cracks the first man inside, off the LOS.

UNBALANCED LINE—TOSS SWEEP

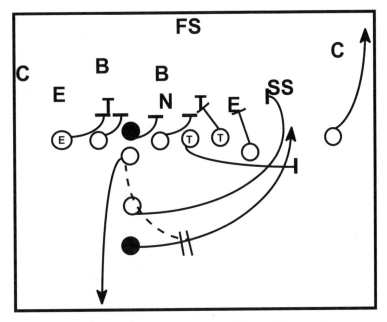

Figure 10-65 Unbalanced Line Toss Sweep

Coaching Points: When we ran an unbalanced line, we brought a tackle over and lined up a tight end on the other side. Teams have to play the backside different if the man on the end of the line is an eligible receiver.

Outside Tackle and Wingback—Block down on first man inside on the LOS.

Inside Tackle—Pull and block first man with odd-color jersey. We tell him to expect contact on his third step.

All Other Linemen—Run an overblock.

Wide Receiver—Push and block corner.

Fullback—Seal tight inside—off wingback's block.

Tailback—Read tackle's block.

Quarterback—Turn, toss to tailback, and walk back ten yards, watching play.

FAKE TOSS SWEEP—FAKE REVERSE—THROWBACK TO TAILBACK

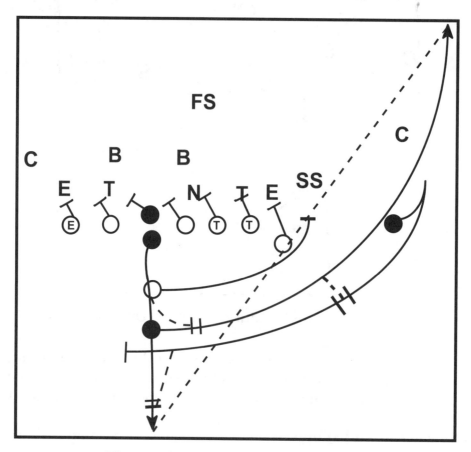

Figure 10–66 Fake Toss Sweep

Coaching Points: Out of the unbalanced line, we ran the toss sweep with a great deal of success. We also ran the reverse and several other of our base plays, according to how the other team adjusted to our unbalanced set. This throwback to the tailback is usually not a play that you would run every week. We would always choose our time, and the only team that ever stopped this particular play was the one who rode on the bus to the game with me. When we did not overthrow the tailback or he didn't drop the pass, the throwback pass resulted in a long gainer or a touchdown.

<u>Entire Line and Wingback</u>—Aggressively block the gap away.

<u>Fullback</u>—Seal first man outside the wingback's block.

<u>Quarterback</u>—After tossing the ball to the tailback, take ten-yard stroll straight back, watching the play.

Tailback—Receive the toss, tuck the ball, and give a good three or four-yard fake upfield. Run inside wide receiver and deliver the ball to him with a "dead" toss. Take a few slow steps, looking back at receiver, and "haul tail" down the sidelines, looking over your inside shoulder.

Wide Receiver—Take two hard steps upfield, plant outside foot, and come behind the tailback. Take the "dead" toss and give a good fake for three or four steps. Then "dead" toss the ball to the quarterback and block any backside trash.

Coaching tip: We coached the offensive line to block for three counts and then all to yell, "Reverse." We found that linebackers and defensive backs can't tell who is doing the yelling, and usually they would react to the fake call.

SPRINT RIGHT—SCREEN TO LEFT END

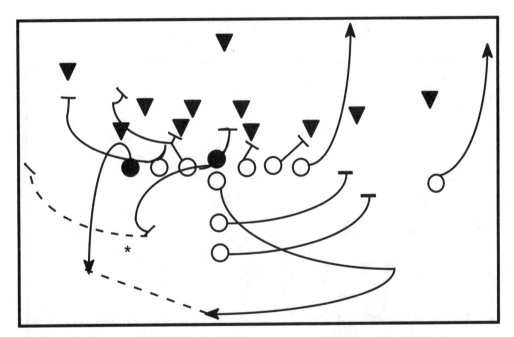

Figure 10-67 Sprint Right—Screen to Left End

Coaching Points: We could run this play from this basic two-tight pro set, twins away from tight end, and sometimes, depending on what kind of pass defense we expected, we lined up in a pro set and motion Z away from the tight end to get the defense to move.

Playside Tackle, Guard, and Center—Basic screen rules—if covered stop the initial charge of defensive man and try to lose him *inside*.
Tackle—pull down line and get outside position on corner force.

Guard—release flat down the line and get position to seal outside linebacker.

Center—position yourself between receiver and quarterback and ensure the catch. *If no defensive player recognizes screen and attacks the receiver—turn and lead the play.

Backside Guard and Tackle—Block #1 and #2 on the LOS.

Tailback and Fullback—Sprint wide and seal contain.

Quarterback—Sprint right, getting depth—continue until challenged—whirl, getting depth, throw on the run.

Left Tight End—Fire out into defensive end and fall to the ground. Get up and *walk* five yards behind LOS. After catch, turn outside and find the tackle's block.

FAKE POWER LEFT—BOOTLEG PICK

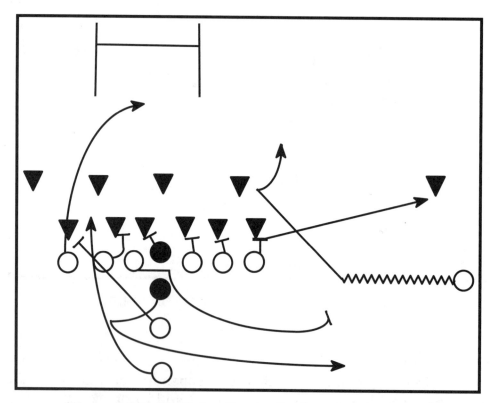

Figure 10-68 Fake Power Left—Bootleg Pick

Coaching Points: We like this play on the goal line on first or second down (sometimes as a two-point play). Two very important points of emphasis on this play are that the wingback must screen the linebacker, being careful not to make contact with him, and then set up facing the quarterback as if running a spot pass. The quarterback was asked this question every time we ran this play in practice, "Had you rather have a ten-dollar bill or a ten-dollar check?" By that we meant that if you reach the corner and there's nothing but grass between you and the goal line, take the "ten-dollar bill" (run the football)—you *know* it's good!

Right End—Block for three counts and release to the flats.

Wingback—Motion and set up in front of the linebacker covering the tight end—**Do Not Touch!**

Right Tackle/Right Guard—Gap away—protect the outside.

Center—Fill for the pulling guard.

Left Guard—Bootleg pull—two flat steps and get depth outside of defensive end.

Left Tackle—Block #2 on the LOS.

Left End—Release and "get open" between the goal posts.

Fullback—Block defensive end.

Tailback—Good fake off tackle unless there are two coming from outside end—then forget fake and block second rusher.

Quarterback—Good fake to tailback—turn and get depth—look to run first. If the run isn't there, first read is for the tight end in the flats. If he is covered, look for the left end between the goal posts.

We worked on this play (with variations shown below) every practice during goal-line offense. We ran it out of two or three different sets, but the basic blocking and reads were always the same. We scored several touchdowns and a few crucial two-point conversions with this play. The following account is about a time that we *did not* score: The setting is a miserable night with a steady rain soaking the field for this final playoff game for the state championship. Late in the fourth quarter, these weather conditions and two good defenses, coupled with mistakes caused by these two factors, had the score at 0–0, but we were threatening on the three-yard line. I have described the events that took place on the second down of this drive, where we were stopped when our "coach-on-the-field" right guard failed to run his overblock for reasons known only by his Maker. So—it's third and goal on the three-yard line. With the state championship on the line, we called timeout and dialed up this play: "Power left bootleg—wingback pick on one—ready break." Please read carefully once more the coaching points that were stressed *every* time we worked on this play. At no time was the quarterback given the option of doing what he did on this play on this night. Let me insert the fact that our wingback was *not* a receiver or a runner—he was just the best blocking back I have ever coached. His job was to free the tight end with his "pick" on the linebacker. As the play developed, it looked as if our side had directed the actions of the players on *both* sides of the ball. When the quarterback rode the tailback in the off-tackle hole to his left, it appeared that the entire defense was headed there to stop our "favorite play." The defensive end who lined up on our right end came inside, leaving our pulling guard with no one to block, so he proceeded to get his depth and head upfield to lead the quarterback into pay dirt with nothing to block but air. As the quarterback came out of his fake, all he saw was grass and a chunky right guard with the same colored jersey turning up toward the goal line. The linebacker assigned to this tight end had left him and was looking to get in on the tackle to his right. Our left end was standing under the goal posts, all by himself, doing the side-straddle hop. With no linebacker to screen, our wingback turned and prepared to watch his quarterback score the state-championship-winning touchdown. The cliché we used to emphasize our main coaching point for this play was emphatically and sadly displayed as the "ten-dollar bill" being handed to our quarterback was spurned for the "ten-dollar check" as he drilled the wingback in the chest with the football. The "check" bounced as the startled wingback watched the unexpected football fall to the inundated turf. A fourth-down chip-shot field goal sailed wide right, and the score was still 0 to 0. This didn't last long. Four plays later, the all-state quarterback of our fired-up opponent, feeding off the momentum gained by this goal-line stand, broke three tackles on an option play and scored on a 67-yard run. A victory for us on that night was just not meant to be.

As mentioned, we ran this basic play with several different looks. I've included the following variations to stimulate your thinking to adapt the play to your offensive philosophy and scheme:

PICK PLAY WITH MOTION

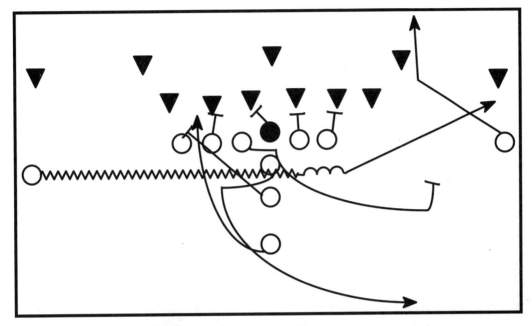

Figure 10–69 Pick Play with Motion

PICK ON BACKSIDE BACKER

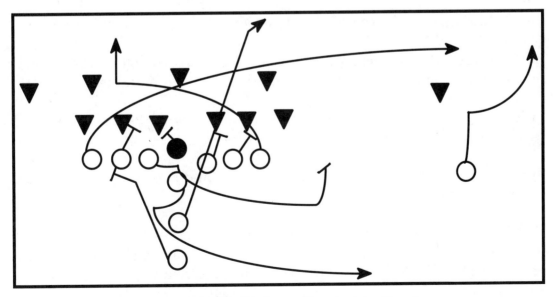

Figure 10–70 Pick on Backside Backer

FAKE FIELD GOAL

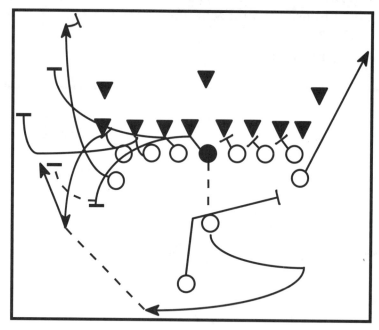

Figure 10–71 Fake Field Goal

Coaching Points: Like most "special plays," you can't run this every game, but when it was appropriate, I found this fake field goal to be very effective.

<u>Right Side Linemen</u>—Block down.

<u>Right Wingback</u>—Release upfield for end zone.

<u>Left Wingback</u>—Release upfield—take corner deep and then block him.

<u>Left Tackle</u>—Regular screen rules. Make contact with defensive man and release down the line, getting outside position on first man inside.

<u>Left Guard</u>—Regular screen rules. Make contact with defensive man and seal to the inside.

<u>Center</u>—Personal protector. Ensure the pass, and if nothing shows—turn and lead the play.

<u>Left End</u>—Make contact with defensive man—try to lose him inside. Retreat five yards behind LOS. Position yourself in an open position between rushers and quarterback. After the catch turn to the outside and pick up blocks.

<u>Kicker</u>—Simulate the kick and then block backside trash.

Holder (Quarterback)—Catch ball and quickly stab it toward the tee. Bring ball to throwing position and sprint to right, looking toward right wingback. Whirl right, getting depth. Find left end and throw on the run.

END-AROUND REVERSE KICKOFF RETURN

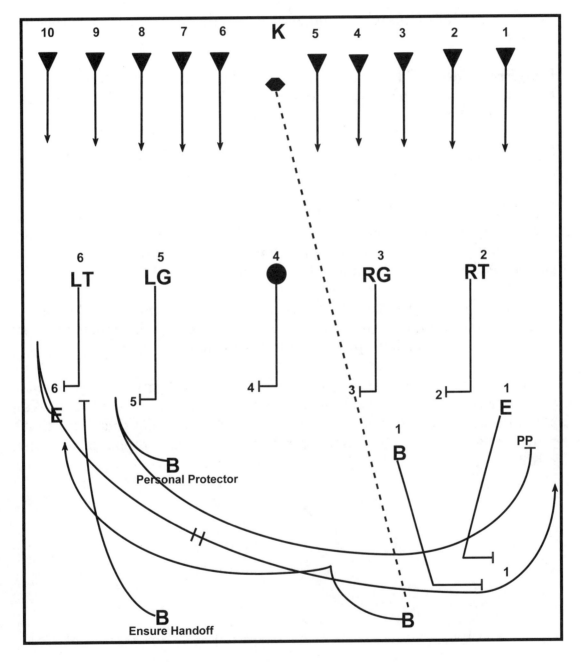

Figure 10–72 End-Around Reverse Kickoff Return

Coaching Points: When we scouted a team and found that they did not stay in their lanes when covering the kickoff, we would work on this return and have it ready just in case we needed it. We worked on the timing many times during the summer practices, and all that was needed during the season was a quick refresher. If we had this return called and the ball went to anyone other than one of the two deep backs, everyone knew that the return became a wedge on the ball.

Right End/Right Upback—Drop toward the middle and merge together to block #1 inside-out.

Five Front Men—Count from playside and block numbers 2–6 outside-in. Drop straight back and allow the coverage to flow toward the fake. (Do not count the kicker.)

Left Upback—Drift toward fake—then turn and lead the play—personal protector.

Deep Backs—The back who receives the kick starts upfield and then finds the other deep back, letting him lead you to the handoff area. Slow down for inside handoff to left end—look it in—then turn and continue upfield with a good fake. The deep back without the ball ensures the handoff.

Left End—We want our best runner lined up at this position. He starts upfield, plants, and comes back inside the deep back with the ball, making a good pocket. Find the left upback and follow his block.

With the proper timing and when run against an aggressive opponent, this return can quickly turn the momentum your way in a close contest. We also ran a fake reverse with some modification in the blocking rules that proved effective after the other team had scouted and prepared for this return.

CHAPTER 11

Offensive Personnel

Selection of Personnel

In high school, coaches are not given the luxury of selecting their players from a list of tried and tested athletes at each position. Often the player who ran over everyone in junior high or peewees did so because he had matured sooner and was bigger and stronger than his peers. By the time these young men reach you, most of the late bloomers have caught up with those who developed early and who have reached their full size by the eighth grade and, in many instances, have passed them. The first problem this presents is one of convincing the big kid who was an offensive stud running back in junior high that he would be a better lineman in high school. Also, many mamas and daddies want their sweet little darling to be the star quarterback or some other high-profile player when their genes just won't allow it. Then there is always the non-athlete whose daddy is president of the booster club. Although these are all genuine problems that must be addressed, the situation is usually as the old dairy farmer said, "The cream will always rise to the top!" The selection of positions must be a *coaching-staff* decision after the first few practices *in pads*. I have seen plenty of *All-Americans* in shorts who turned out to be second and third-string backups when we went full blow in pads. Also, it must be noted that these positions are not set in stone. As players continue to grow and mature, their contributions to the team may need to be adjusted accordingly. I have tried to be as flexible as possible in this selection process but also firm, always considering what is best for the team rather than for only the individual. That takes us back to that selling job. If you have been successful in that most important aspect of your position, both players and their parents will respect your decision for the betterment of the team. The following comments include some of the attributes that I *looked* for and *hoped* for (but didn't always get) at the different positions:

Quarterbacks

Wherever you are coaching, at whatever level, the first player to consider if you are going to have success is the quarterback. If you have moved into a new job, it may be that the fellow who lined up there for the other coach is not the guy to run *your* package. It may take an assessment of all the candidates before you choose *your* leader of the team. As you assess those capable of playing this important position, you have to compare what you *want them to do* versus what they *can do*. Can they run? Pass? Do both? Do we need two—a runner and a passer? A very important part of this process is often overlooked; that is, there is more to filling this position than pure athletic ability that can be measured with a stopwatch and a tape measure. The subsequent observations should help to expand your appraisal:

Solomon's admonition to parents concerning the rearing of our children *"Train up a child in the way he should go: and when he is old, he will not depart from it"* (Proverbs 22:6) gives us inspired assistance in this important but sometimes difficult task with our own offspring. We can respectfully and seriously apply these same words from the Bible to the way a good quarterback *should* have been taught. The development of a quarterback *should* start at an early age with the teaching of proper fundamentals and techniques. This means putting emphasis on "the little things." As the "good quarterback" matures, he will not depart from those "little things" taught to him at a younger age. During football season this axiom is displayed every Sunday afternoon when one watches the "good 'uns" play on the tube. These "little things" include carrying out the fake, looking off the defender, having "happy feet" in the pocket, and being a leader on and off the field. I believe that the *most* important trait to look for in a quarterback is this leadership ability, which involves being able to take plenty of criticism or to "take the blame." To me this attribute emphasizes the real meaning of what a leader has to be. I coached a very talented young quarterback back in the early '70s. This young man won a lot of games for us with his playing skills, but what I remember most about him is his use of these two words: "My fault!" These words usually did not hold the truth concerning the situation for which they were used. This exceptional player had a sterling attitude and had never forgotten what happened on the very first day of practice. He had fumbled a snap from center and was coaching him on how to bring the ball up and hit his upper hand. I interrupted his coaching debut and informed him where the entire neighborhood could hear it: "It's *always* the quarterback's fault!" To be the leader that he should be, your quarterback must be able to take the blame and to share the credit. This leadership quality *should* be instilled into the mind of every quarterback from an early age. If this is *not* the case with the list of candidates you've been given, your first coaching task *must* be to start the process to instill this quality in your team leader.

Offensive Line

The ideal offensive lineman is 6'5", weighs 300 pounds, and runs a 4.8 forty. (Unfortunately, he also plays for the Seattle Seahawks.) Naturally, these are the characteristics that we would like to see displayed in our five "big hawgs," but after we realize that this type player comes along very seldom, especially in high school, we still have to field a team on Friday night. These folks are a very important cog in that winning wheel. What we *do* look for in our linemen *is* a certain degree of size, but if they are going to be able to do the things well that we ask them to do, it is imperative that they have quickness and what we all call "good feet." This means that we will forego the guy with a 280-pound frame, who can't walk and chew gum at the same time, for a 220-pounder who can maintain his block with the good balance provided by proper footwork. We constantly work on this phase of blocking throughout the off-season with jump ropes, spot drills, and other drills of quickness and coordination that train the feet of these bigger guys through constant repetition.

We strive to teach each lineman every position for basically two reasons: First, this will ensure that we always have the best personnel in the game, and, second, because of the various blocking calls our linemen make, it is essential that they know the total blocking scheme. As mentioned, in most high school situations, good offensive linemen *are* at a premium. After the decision is made regarding the starting five, there are usually two or three who are only a notch below the starters. If you designate a position to each player ("You're a guard, you're a tackle..."), and an injury occurs to the right guard but your next best lineman is "a tackle," you end up with a player in the game who is not the best. This coaching technique proved to be very valuable but also devastating one year when we were undefeated and playing in the state-championship game. As is typical of a long, hard season, we had several nagging injuries to some key linemen going into the game, but we still had available one very good "utility" player who knew every position on the offensive line, including center and tight end. During this fight for the state title, this young man played every position on the line, *including* center and tight end. It can be truthfully said that he knew the offense as well as any coach on the field that night. Having said all of that, I have no explanation for his only minus of the night that occurred on third down on the two-yard line on a play that should have scored the touchdown that would have put the blue trophy in *our* case rather than in our opponent's. The call was a simple power play off-tackle—block down, kick out, and lead through—everyone runs it. The team we were playing lined up in a 6–5 goal-line defense with the entire defensive line with their butts up in the air in a goal-line charge. We knew that if any action came their way, the inside backers would charge through the B gap on the side we ran. Our blocking scheme was designed to stop this penetration with a simple overblock, getting our head past the charging linebacker and thus keeping him on his side of the line of scrimmage. Our young man was lined up at right guard, and the play was called. "Power Right on one." The line fired off in unison and reestablished the line of scrimmage two yards deep in the end zone. The minus came when this blocking machine—this football sponge—didn't run the overblock to the right but instead blocked down on the A gap player, leaving a straight shot for the linebacker to meet the tailback head-on two yards deep in our backfield. When asked why he did it, there were no excuses given, just a simple and very humble "I don't know, Coach." One might say that at this point, our coaching technique had backfired on us and that we had put too much pressure on this young man to learn and to perform at too many positions. The truth is that without this young man and the knowledge that he had soaked up through hours of coaching and dedicated practice, we would never have been in a position to even *compete* for that trophy.

Tight Ends

In many of the modern-day offenses, this position has become a "dinosaur," but to have the type of offense that is compatible in *all* situations, a versatile tight end is a *must*. The first and most important quality that we look for in this important player is blocking skills. Ideally, this unique player will possess the size and the blocking attributes of a tackle with the speed and pass-catching ability of a wide receiver. If he does and can score high on the ACT, he'll need to enlarge the size of his mailbox, for good tight ends are still a premium at the college level—and above. When we coach this position, we work him with both the offensive line and the receivers. If we notice that in certain situations you play our tight end man with your linebacker, we *will* slip in a receiver at that position, trying to develop a mismatch for the linebacker.

Receivers

To state the obvious, the primary attribute we look for in our receivers is the ability to catch the football. We also insist that they be willing and able to block downfield on our running plays. The task of convincing them to perfect this skill is made easier when we show them how open they become on our play-action passes when we have a successful running game. We work a lot with our receivers on *how* to run their routes. Precise routes and pass-catching ability will often compensate for the lack of speed at the receiver position. In high school, a receiver often has to double as a defensive back. If this is the case, the receiver will know the keys that the defensive back coach has told him to look for if he is guarding someone. For instance, in man-to-man coverage we tell the defensive back to watch the receiver's eyes. A subtle head fake and what we call "the big eye" will often cause the man coverage to "bite" and to result in a completed pass. If this is not the case, we have our receivers meet with the defense and take time to study the defensive back's techniques so that they can better run their routes.

Running Backs

Size, speed, and agility are all attributes that we would like to have in every player who lines up in our backfield. Realistically, in high school we are lucky if we have one player who possesses even two of these three traits. While size and speed are God-given qualities, a certain degree of agility can be attained through a regiment of drills. There are other factors that are found in the really good backs: toughness, the ability to read and set up blocks, and certainly endurance. I have found that, for me at least, the best all-around drill to teach these skills is a well-organized, controlled scrimmage. By well-organized I mean that it shows the backs the various blocking patterns used against an assortment of defenses that they must read and adjust to. A controlled scrimmage is one in which at least one of the coaches is watching the *play* and not the *players* so that he can execute a quick whistle to minimize injuries.

Throughout my coaching days, I have been blessed to stand on the sidelines and to watch some very talented young men "tote the mail." The best I've seen? You won't find his name in any record book. I have no newspaper clippings recording his phenomenal feats to show you. I can't show you any film on this amazing back, but I "*garrantee*" that if you could see footage of him, he would be high on *your* list of all-time best players at this position too. The first year of integration in the state of Alabama is the setting. A group of very talented black players is reassigned to an all-white school with all-white coaches. The young man in question declares himself a running back and produces a ragged school annual and a scrapbook showing himself to be a starter as an eighth grader for an all-black school in another state. "That's good, son, but this is Alabama, and we play football down here." I didn't say that to this fellow, but I'm sure that I thought it. After the allotted days in shorts, it was obvious that this new guy *did* possess the last two of those qualities I mentioned—he was fast and he was agile. "He won't be able to produce when we get the pads on and he gets smacked in the face," was the consensus of the entire staff as we discussed our newly acquired prospect. Fifteen minutes into the first scrimmage, after watching the defense grab air each time he carried the ball, it was quite obvious that "We were wrong!" would be a gross understatement. I don't remember his ever being tackled in that scrimmage. Not only was he doing things that I had never seen on any high school football field, but he was giving coaching tips to his awe-stricken teammates. I wish that this Cinderella story could end at the big dance with our riding off in a big pumpkin—but not so. One week before the first game, after we had already dusted off a spot in our trophy case for that blue one, we got the bad news. The secretary called me to the office and informed me that she had received the transcripts from the dismantled black school and that our star running back had repeated the ninth grade and didn't have any eligibility left. He took this news a whole lot better than the coaches did and asked if he could stay out there with us and help us coach his ex-teammates. We gladly agreed, and I'll have to say that his coaching ability was almost as amazing as his playing skills. (Don't hang up yet!) There was a young assistant coach from a prominent OVC college by the name of Mickey Andrews who was recruiting our area at the time. On his first visit he asked if we had anyone that he would be interested in. "Not playing," I told him. "We're rebuilding and real young, but I've got one here that's ineligible to play for us. If you sign him, he'll make you famous." He *did* sign him, and he called me after their first game to tell us "the *good* news and the *bad* news." The *good* news was that he *was* all that I said he was. He had taken the opening kickoff in the opening ball game one yard deep in the end zone, and one hundred one yards later, he slammed the ball to the turf to the elation of a stadium full of astonished fans and some very excited coaches. The *bad* news was that in the very next series, he sustained a career-ending knee injury that I'm convinced kept his bust out of that big building in Canton, Ohio.

Part X

After the Final Whistle

CHAPTER 12

Off-Season Program

Evaluation

Always, for me, the last handshake at mid-field signaled the beginning of another football season. As soon as the season was over, I started thinking about what I was going to do the *next* season. Although I always gave the *team* a week or two to recoup, *coaches who win* are not afforded that luxury. During that intermission for the team, the coaches would meet to set up an off-season program based on the availability and needs of players. Before we could organize a meaningful off-season program, an in-depth evaluation of all returning personnel was conducted. This evaluation process must involve all the coaches, JV as well as varsity. Our first item for discussion was the returning starters. The strengths and the weaknesses of each player were gone over, and a tentative decision was made concerning his potential contribution to next year's team. First to be considered in this process are the players who might need to make a position change and the special preparation involved in such a change. For example, I always like to have my best lineman at the center position and my best athlete at quarterback. These are two positions that take more than a pat on the butt and the declaration to "Get in there and play center (or quarterback)." If the center position is being vacated by graduation, an immediate decision must be made concerning his replacement. This could be as simple as penciling in his backup, or if that choice is questionable, we decide on another lineman who has the size and the athletic ability to be taught this very important position. The center position is much like that of quarterback—you had better have three ready to go at the opening kickoff of each game. When I say "ready to go," I mean that you should have at least three players who can line up at quarterback, take a snap, and run your basic plays—and three players who can make that snap. We always had several linemen working year-round on this component of that important position. (I have never been able to draw up an offensive play without a "hiker and a hikee.") The center-quarterback exchange (whether shotgun or hands-on-butt) is a phase of the game that should be worked on every day in the off-season. If an inexperienced lineman is being considered for the center position—be patient. I have always said that playing and coaching the offensive line are the two most difficult and most important aspects of the game. We ask these fellows to run into what are usually the biggest and meanest players on the opposing team and to push them in a direction that they do not want to go—admittedly, a very difficult assignment for anyone. For the center to do this and at the same time deliver the ball to a teammate with one arm between his legs complicates the task even more. It will take hours of dedicated practice to perfect this procedure, so again, be patient.

In most instances, the quarterback's departure will involve a thorough assessment of all the available candidates. Above all other positions, this is one that must be *earned* and not *inherited*. I mentioned the prerequisite of being "my best athlete." This term demands a definition. Your "best athlete" can't always be established based on his forty time or where his name rests on the weight-lifting charts. Although these tangible things are important at any position, there are other *intangible* characteristics that are discussed and confirmed before any name goes under this most important heading. I have already discussed the attributes that I look for in this "field general." If you look back and check, you'll see that topping the criteria is leadership. This quality must be recognized not only by the coaching staff but also—and especially—by his teammates. It has been my experience through the years that the young man who fills this leadership role on the playing field on Friday night usually displays these qualities in the classroom and in all other areas of his life.

After reaching a consensus on these two positions, our discussion is focused on the remaining individual positions and the experience (or lack of) at each. As a tentative depth chart is produced, be sure that the coaches and the players whose names are on that list understand the term *tentative*. There are many factors that can change that list in the course of seven or eight months: dedication, growth spurts, attitude adjustments (positive and negative), grades, new additions to our community, and sometimes topping the list is the discovery of that special little "sweet thing." As a means of curtailing the complacency that might be produced by a favorable placement on the depth chart, we try to have an element of competition in everything we do in the off-season. Every player has strengths and weaknesses. The entire staff is involved in the production of this two-sided list for each player. We try to develop a program that will increase those strengths and eliminate those weaknesses. The players who buy into our program *will* get better— how much depends on *them*. We keep a chart on everything: weight gain, weight loss, forty time, shuttle time, all of our lifts, and for our specialty players (snappers, punters, kickers, receivers, quarterbacks), a daily log showing how many times they have practiced their specialty. These charts are a visible tool that we use to encourage our players (especially the weaker ones) as their names move up with improvement in each category. I have also found that even the stronger, more experienced athlete is motivated as he sees the dedicated, determined "no name" at his position begin to inch up with each passing evaluation. If you're a coach who has the luxury of two-platooning, be sure that the placement of potential personnel is balanced on both sides of the ball. I have seen coaches who were orientated to either offense or defense load up on one side or the other and, consequently, not be able to score or to keep the other team from scoring.

Still another very important item of discussion during this evaluation process, which too is often overlooked by some coaches for one reason or another, concerns the adjustment of their offensive or defensive scheme to the returning personnel. As I have already discussed, with an established program that involves every feeder school, there should be very few adjustments. But if your personnel pool is sparse, I have found that it is much easier for you to adjust what *you* do than to try to suddenly produce athletes to continue running an offense or executing a defensive scheme that they are physically unable to accomplish. For example, if I'm fortunate enough to have a quarterback who can run and is tough, I'm going to run some sort of option offense. Any defensive coach will tell you that stopping a good option team is one of the hardest assignments that he has. The "good" part of that description will not apply if the fellow taking the snap can't run the football. If that option guy has graduated and after we filter through our choices and are convinced that there's no one available who can do all that we ask of that position with our present offense, we have only two choices. We can either be dogmatic and continue to run what we always have, or we can adjust our plan to suit the abilities of the returning players. Coaches who do not feel comfortable coaching anything but "what I've always run" usually implement the first of these choices. There have been numerous times that my staff and I have driven hundreds of miles to sit and listen to some college coach instruct us in the installation of a particular offense that we feel is better suited to our personnel.

The same thing is true on the other side of the football. I have described the two types of defenses that I like to employ—stunting and reading. If I have the appropriate personnel, I will run both, for I have discovered through the years that it takes different blocking techniques to be effective against one verses the other. This involves more coaching and creates confusion on the offensive line. I also realize that if my defensive linemen are not big and strong, but rather small and quick, I better not ask them to line up and read a 260-pound tackle. If this is the case, we will work a lot on jitterbugging and stunting the down-linemen to free our linebackers. Speaking of linebackers—if the evaluation process produces only three players capable of playing this most important defensive position, we don't need to depend on stopping folks with a plan that involves four or five. I firmly believe that these evaluation sessions and the implementation of their conclusions have contributed considerably to any success that I have had in winning football games.

Individual Meetings

In the old days, I knew coaches who didn't see their players, except accidentally, from the end of May until the start of summer practice in late August. I always tried throughout the entire summer to keep in contact with those guys who played for me. I didn't want them to forget me nor replace me with some other extra-curricular activity—one that wore lipstick! Summer schedules, for both players and coaches, must be discussed before the last school bell rings. In modern-day football, those who coach it and those who play it must realize that just to remain competitive involves an off-season commitment to do whatever it takes to get better. Position coaches will need to set up individual meetings with the personnel for which they are responsible. The offensive linemen will need to walk through and learn every block that they will be asked to make against every defense that they will face the next year. The *little things* that are involved in proper blocking techniques, such as the appropriate splits, first step, and the use of his hands, can be learned without the use of pads and headgear. We want our offensive backs and their coach to attend these sessions with the offensive line in order to learn the blocking schemes on each play. If they learn the various calls (and how they will be executed) made by the linemen for each play, it helps them to better read the defense and increases their yards per carry. In sessions with the defensive line coach, these players can be taught their alignments on each of our defenses and how to jitterbug from one to another. Defensive backs learn adjustments to different sets and how to disguise coverage, along with their proper mechanics, through many sessions and drills with their position coach. I have mentioned all of these seemingly obvious off-season practices to lead up to this statement: I never "wasted" time in the short period allotted by the state that we call spring training in teaching line splits, proper steps, correct alignment, or in learning plays. During that time we worked on what we all know really wins ball games—blocking and tackling (more on this later).

There are two groups of players to whom we always allotted extra time for more in-depth teaching—quarterbacks and linebackers. With the returning quarterbacks or with those who were competing for that position the next year, we would sit down and go over every game film and critique each play. I forgot to mention that one prerequisite that one must possess to apply for this job as quarterback: thick skin. It is during these one-on-one film sessions that I (or the offensive coordinator) will deliver the most scathing *constructive* criticism directed toward my team leader. Although he is *coached* the year round, I try not to risk destroying his confidence nor the team's confidence in *him* during the season with belittling remarks made in front of his teammates. We tell our quarterback, "Never run a bad play." We equip him with a simple audible process that will enable him to check out of any play we call that has a low percentage of being successful against the defense he sees as he walks toward the LOS. With that being said, it is imperative that we transfer as much knowledge from *our* minds to *his* as possible. We have our quarterback review each game film with the offensive coordinator and to make decisions on every play until he understands (or at least has a general idea) what we want to run out of each set against various defenses. In these sessions we really concentrate on our four or five toughest opponents.

Just as important to the success of our team is the knowledge that our linebacker crew has concerning the opponents they will face. Our defensive coordinator meets with these players on a regular basis throughout the off-season, reviewing films and allowing them to realize the procedure that we use in establishing a defensive game plan for each opponent. An important aspect of this procedure is developing an understanding of the other team's offensive game plan and how they intended to attack our defense. First of all, we decide what they must consider to be their best five or six "go-to" plays. We want every linebacker to be able to adjust our defense to an alignment that, when executed properly, should stop these plays. My philosophy has always been—if we can stop what they do best, we make them do stuff they haven't practiced as much. All coaches have tendencies. As we review the films with our linebackers, we assist them in deciding the tendencies of each coach we face. Do they run most plays toward their bench? Are they right-handed or left-handed? Does the fullback always lead the play? Do they flip-flop certain linemen? Who is their go-to back or lineman? These are just a few of the things that we have them try to pick out from each film that they review.

These off-season sessions with our leaders on both sides of the ball have always been an important part of our teaching process essential to having a winning program. *We want our quarterbacks and linebackers to become an extension of the coach on the field.* Every coach must remember that it's not what *we* know that's important but how much the *combatants* on the field know and how well *they* can execute.

Goal Setting

I've always been a big advocate of goal setting. I realize that this is a component of every coach's on-going motivational dialogue with his team. Although there should always be two sets of goals—personal and team oriented—in a team sport such as football, it is virtually impossible to separate the two. Personal or individual goals, to have significance in our overall plan, must be sincere, realistic, and measurable. This important aspect of coaching must be a mutual endeavor with both the athlete and the coach contributing to the final list. Teenagers, when left to establish their own goals, have a tendency to do one of two things: They either set unrealistic, unattainable objectives, which usually lead to a quick departure from their efforts, or they establish goals that are so vague that they can't be evaluated.

When each team member is dedicated to the attaining of a well-thought-out list of realistic goals, then the desired team goals can be established. Team goals do not differ that much from those of each team member although to be realistic, they must be flexible. This may seem inconsistent, but if the first team goal listed is to go undefeated and you run out of time in the first ball game and *undefeated* is no longer achievable, there must be other attainable goals in order to maintain the motivation desired. One obvious goal will involve those players who need to either lose weight or gain weight. Either one of these goals is very attainable, and as with all of us, it is simple—diet and exercise. The exercise part of this equation is much easier than the diet part. Your established weight and exercise program will be posted and closely supervised by the coaches, but the diet of your athletes depends on Mama and the individual involved. A set of scales and a weight chart that is also closely monitored should help encourage those athletes who struggle with weight problems (either too much or too little) to improve through a structured diet.

Strength Training

There are as many strength programs available as there are college weight coaches. I believe that weight training is a lot like going on a diet. Most diets are good if you stick to them faithfully and don't cheat. The same is true of tested weight programs. The success of any strength plan is the attitude and the work ethic of the guys involved in it. This includes both the participating players and the coaches assigned to implement it. When I began coaching, hardly anyone, including most of the college teams, had a well-organized, mandatory weight program. I can remember the time when the coaches told me not to touch those weights. "They'll make you muscle bound," they said. I never did much weight lifting myself, but at the first school where I had a head-coaching job, I probably had the first weight-lifting program in that neck of the woods. Although it was not as sophisticated as the computerized ones that are available today, I sold the players on what we did, and they *did* get stronger. In fact, they were so sold on this *innovative procedure* that the time or two I had to go out of town and forgot to leave them a key for the old shed where we kept the weights, they took the door off the hinges so they wouldn't miss their valuable workouts. I believe that this, coupled with a lot of hard work and a group of dedicated athletes who were hungry to win, significantly contributed to the undefeated season my first year there. It was several years before most coaches finally wised up and realized that "Bigger—Stronger—Faster" would win more games. I was in my twelfth year of coaching when a relative of one of my assistants came to visit him over the Christmas holidays. This fine fellow was the starting running back for the national champions and was drafted by the NFL. My assistant brought him to the gym during one of our weight workouts, and our

190-pound linebacker challenged him to a bench-press contest. This linebacker was doing reps with 250 pounds and maxed out at about 310. This college (soon-to-be NFL) running back struggled to get 165. Times *surely* have changed!

Regardless of which weight program you settle on, there is one imperative ingredient that, if left out, will render your efforts one degree above useless— INTENSITY! I have visited coaches on my schedule during their off-season and witnessed weight workouts that could have passed for a school picnic had it not been for the heaps of scrap iron in the way. I would leave—looking forward to the time that we would line up against them and *rain on their little picnic*. The first element (and maybe the most important) of a profitable weight program is coaches who are *completely* sold on the program and will accept nothing less than total, concentrated effort from everyone involved. *Their* intensity and enthusiasm are quickly passed on to the impressionable teenagers that they are training. The second important factor that is necessary for the desired outcome of the program is *organization*. This of course begins with a comprehensive evaluation of each player in order to place him with a group who has similar abilities. Although my practice schedules may not be as rigid as some, I *do* realize that to adequately train seventy or eighty young men, in what is many times an inadequate space, there must be a systematic plan that is strictly followed by all participants. An important part of this organizational plan will involve coordinating your summer workouts with the inevitable summer jobs that most of the players will have. This goes back to the Wal-Mart concept of coaching—expect to come early and to stay late.

Skill Training

When those of us in the football world discuss "skill players," we normally think of quarterbacks, receivers, and running backs. While these athletes must possess certain God-given abilities—speed, quickness, agility, size—we as coaches still must be able to recognize and develop these talents. I have always heard it said that there are two things you can't coach: size and speed. It's true. Mama and Daddy and a good gene pool are responsible for the existence of the basics of these two attributes. Yet through the years there have been drills and programs designed by coaches and other specialists in the field of physical training that can enhance that speed, and your weight program and diet can make some adjustments to the size factor. By the definition given, improving the skills of these players involves throwing, catching, and running—and plenty of it.

This day and time, there are as many different types of summer football camps as there are positions on the team. When these are available, the wise coach will encourage those he's counting on in the fall to enlist in as many as possible. Not only are these camps beneficial for the development of particular skills, but they also keep the thought process of the athlete focused on the upcoming season—the outcome of which decides the success of the team—and the security of *your job*.

Spring Training

As I have alluded to previously, preparation for what is labeled and set aside as your formal "spring training" must begin in the winter months immediately after you watch the seniors depart the field for the last time. In fact, I usually had next year's lineup scratched on several pieces of scrap paper lying around the house and office even before the current season was over. I've always tried to avoid interfering with my players who were involved in other sports, but I did try to maintain a relationship with my team leaders that generally got more intimate as the leaves started to turn green. I have never been a "stingy coach." By that statement I mean this: I have always had the philosophy that if a young man has the ability and desire to participate in all sports, he should. These will always be your best athletes and are usually those at the skill positions. Coaches of other sports who pressure athletes to "concentrate" on *their* sport are doing those athletes a real injustice. I have listened to the arguments that declare that if this one or that one would just apply himself solely to *that* coach's sport, his chances of signing a scholarship would be greatly improved. I've always replied to that with this time-tested reasoning: "The guys out there who do all of this recruiting are real good at it—you can't hide a good one!" At most every place I've coached, my quarterback and some of the other skilled players also played baseball, and if they were pretty good and made the playoffs, their season would continue right through spring training. If that was the case, I never meddled with or discouraged my players or the coach involved but rather tried to make every playoff game and encouraged the rest of the team to be there and root for their buddies. It was always my experience with athletes who were talented and dedicated enough to play all sports that they would come early or stay late in order to do the things necessary to contribute. I always used this situation as an opportunity to work with the backups and to work on the fundamentals that win games anyway—blocking and tackling.

If your off-season program is what it should be, conditioning shouldn't be a part of the few days allotted you by the state athletic association for spring training. We always had a good stretching and warm-up session, but most of the periods were devoted to fundamentals and evaluating personnel. The basic fundamentals of winning football games will always remain the same. If you can't block and tackle, you better buy a trailer and tell your own kids not to make any close friends "…'cause you ain't gonna be there long." Although the fundamentals don't change, trends and philosophies are as plentiful and varying as there are successful coaches on the level just above you. It has already been established that coaches are the biggest thieves and copycats on the planet. They'll take the play you beat them with one year, polish it up a little bit, give it another name, and "whup your tail" with it the next. I've done that very same thing many times, but the mistake that many coaches make is trying to run somebody else's stuff *without* somebody else's material. Not only is spring training a time to teach blocking and tackling, but it is the time to polish that evaluation of *your* material and to adapt what *you* do to suit *their* talent or lack of it. "Off-Tackle John" likes to play smashmouth, coming-right-at-you power football, but in high school we have to line up with what Mama and Daddy send us. "Plays don't win football games—players do." This old football axiom is one that we all have heard and whose veracity has never been questioned, but believe me, you won't win many football games running power off-tackle with 200-pound linemen and 150-pound backs. Usually the changes made do not—*and should not*—involve a total makeover of both the offensive and defensive playbooks. Your blocking schemes and defensive philosophy should be flexible enough to allow for the necessary changes to accommodate the addition or depletion of certain aspects of your game plan on both sides of the ball. If the guys you are blessed with have all the attributes I've outlined for the ideal players at each position, it won't matter what you line up in, offensively or defensively. Just get them in shape, give them a schedule, tell them what time the game starts, and let your wife call plays. This *not* being the case, of course, adjustments are usually a necessity. Like everything else in the game of football, these adjustments are primarily *team-based* decisions. It should be noted that any team performs better when the individual players on that team are having success with whatever assignments you have given them. This assessment process not only involves assuring yourself and the other coaches that you aren't asking an individual or the team to perform tasks that are definitely *above* their skill level, but also it is imperative that you let your skilled athletes display their talents. For example, I've seen coaches who were so inflexible in what they did offensively that they would line up a quarterback who could run and throw with the best of them but then have him turn and toss the ball to a less-talented tailback ninety percent of the time. Of course, sometimes this is a product of a coach who is either unwilling or afraid to admit his limitations and turn that part of the game plan over to a more knowledgeable member of his staff. I have mentioned concentrating on my five or six toughest opponents. During the spring we have certain days we name after these opponents. We tell our team that today is Team X Day and that we are running Team X's plays and defenses. If they have certain returning players that we feel we must stop, we'll dress out a scout player in that guy's jersey to emphasize this.

Summertime

I have always thought that the most crucial time in a coach's life is that period from when the last school bell rings in May until the last bold X is marked before the big red circle on his August calendar. It's during this critical time that I have seen the most drastic changes in that tentative depth-chart generated by the coaches after their extensive evaluation process during the off-season and spring training. Wise coaches realize that the "long hot summer" can change that depth-chart and that they must have a contingency plan for one or all of the following circumstances: grades, girls, cars, Allied Van Lines, and "a better offer."

Grades

I have already discussed the monitoring of your athletes' grades on a weekly basis during the entire school year. This procedure, along with the peer tutorial program that I described, should for the most part sidetrack any eligibility problems concerning grades. Invariably, there will be some who will slip through the cracks and have need of a summer school program. That monitoring process should have already alerted you to those who will need to continue their education right through the summer months. The young men who require this remedial service are obviously not your most intellectual nor the most scholastically dedicated members of your squad; therefore, it is still imperative that you continue to supervise these fellows to ensure their eligibility next fall. I try not to leave anything to chance, so depending on the school system, it may be necessary for you to locate the site of the nearest appropriate summer school program. In the past I have been blessed to have competent and concerned counselors to assist these young men and me in making sure that all bases pertaining to their eligibility are covered. Remember that it's still up to you and your coaches to stay on top of the progress (or lack of it) of these fellows to make sure that they earn the appropriate grade necessary to maintain eligibility. It may become necessary to enlist one of those peer tutors, so keep that list handy.

Girls

There is a certain age when young men's hormones really start to erupt. That age may differ with the individual, but invariably, erupt they will. Suddenly, that silly, skinny little pest that he has avoided all these years starts to round out and to smell a whole lot better, and just as suddenly, the "ol' coach" and his teammates move down a notch on his list of priorities. Don't think that I'm going to write two or three paragraphs on this subject and alleviate all the problems associated with those cute little members of the opposite sex. If I had the pat answer to this particular distraction, I would be famous! I did discover years ago that trying to stop this natural process, created by God in the Garden of Eden, is not only futile, but sometimes, if forced to make a choice, your star athlete's decision is not what you bargained for. You and your football team can't compete against Mother Nature. I finally discovered that my only hope was to use my recruiting skills on this "little darling" and try to convince her that this mean old coach is not out to break up her budding romance and try to win her over to my program. I learned the names of these sweet things and would speak to them with friendly remarks such as "Suzy, you know that we've got a big game tomorrow night, and I'm counting on you to make sure that Billy's mama tucks him in bed by 10 o'clock." Girlfriends are inevitable. By making them a positive rather than a negative, your chances of keeping your athletes focused on Friday night rather than on Saturday night will improve tremendously.

Cars

Still another very significant event in the lives of your players that could prove to be harmful to your program is the day they start that sixteenth year of life. This day also represents one of the parents' most dreaded moments. When a sixteen-year-old high-strung, healthy male suddenly has a set of wheels at his disposal, for everyone who is associated with him, life changes. That includes you as his coach. Of course, the most obvious concern is the danger involved in driving a vehicle, especially for an "invincible" teenager. As his coach, about all you can do is the same thing Mama and Daddy do—give him a daily dose of "Be Carefuls." I was never a coach who took advantage of my captive audience during the "everybody-ups," keeping them there on one knee for thirty minutes. I *did* use this time to make some sincere admonitions concerning grades, respecting their mamas and daddies, their teachers, their girlfriends—and not to behave like fools in their automobiles.

Allied Van Lines

There is an old joke we coaches tease each other with when we lose an important game (which actually is every one of them). We say we hate to look out our window in the morning because we're afraid we'll see an Allied Van Lines truck backing into our driveway. I've never had one of these back into *my* driveway, but once or twice I have had a career change by a daddy to cause a drastic change in our lineup for the next season. As coaches, all we can do is treat this like a broken leg or some other season-ending injury that inevitability will occur from time to time. When this happened to me, I would congratulate the daddy and the backup on their promotions and work like the dickens with that backup. Successful coaches had better expect the unexpected, whether pre-season or during the game itself, and be prepared to deal with it. An important part of our coaches' meetings (pre-season or prior to each game) was the discussion of the all-important question "What if?" "Be Prepared," the motto of the Boy Scouts, is some of the soundest advice you can give (or receive) in any phase of your life. In my job (coaching football games) or in the events surrounding the rest of my life, my philosophy has always been "Expect the worst—hope for the best—deal with the worst—be thankful for the best."

Better Offer

I've used the analogy of comparing coaching to selling automobiles. A good salesman (of any product) has to be convinced—or at least convince *you*—that what he has is the best there is and that *you* need it. Football should be an easy sell if *you*, as the salesman, present the product correctly. I've had many motivational placards hanging on my dressing-room wall, but there is one that you not only must convince your players of, but you must also daily display *your* adherence to its message: FOOTBALL IS FUN—ENJOY YOURSELF. Any successful coach can attest to the fact that coaching football—the way it *should* be done—*is* hard work. The truth of that statement can't be denied, but at the same time, when that hard work ceases to be pleasurable and rewarding for you—find another job. This is sound advice that I have given to many coaches throughout my career, but we must remember that this same "fun" concept must be maintained in those under your tutorage every day, or they *will* look for "a better offer." That offer can come in many different packages. A couple that are extremely enticing to these young men I have already mentioned—girls and automobiles. The pleasure associated with that first puppy love goes without any explanation. Even at my age I can still remember *that* feeling. I talked about cars and the danger involved with that independent feeling that a sixteen-year-old boy has with a 250-horsepower machine in his control. What I failed to mention, at least with many of the fellows I've coached, is the responsibility that many parents expect in return for the use of that machine. This usually involves some means of contributing a portion of the expenses connected with that vehicle—a part-time job. With these two enticing "carrots," girls and cars, along with many others dangling before our prospective athlete, you, as his coach, had better ensure that the product that you're hawking is very appealing. Of course, a huge part of the appeal of any endeavor is success. Winning football games and the gratifying feeling associated with triumph over a worthy opponent are big portions of the pleasure sought by both coach and player. (Now, let's go back to my car salesman analogy.) It's pretty easy to make sales if your merchandise consists of nothing but shiny, "souped-up" sports cars, but if your lot is filled with run-down, beat-up jalopies, you had better have a silver tongue and no aversion to lying. I've seen many young coaches lose some potentially really good athletes to that "other option" (whatever it might be) with undesirable coaching tactics used mostly out of frustration or sometimes immaturity that would appeal to no one. I'm not saying that we have to sugarcoat our explanation of flagrant and consistent errors made by our players. It's somewhat like the old story of the two farmers discussing how to handle their stubborn mules. The first farmer hitched his mule to a big stump that they were removing to clear some new ground, and as expected, the mule balked. He laid back his ears and refused to move. The farmer started to yell and to cuss at the unresponsive animal, but he still didn't move. The second farmer spoke up and said, "That ain't the way you do it. You gotta be gentle with your mule." They unhitched the first mule, and the second farmer hitched up his mule. "Giddy up, mule." No response. Then this second old farmer reached down and picked up a two-by-four lying on the ground and hit his mule right between the eyes. The mule's knees buckled, and he hit the ground. The first farmer was amazed at this action and exclaimed loudly to farmer number two, "I thought you said you had to treat him gently." The old mule wobbled up and shook his head. Then, the second farmer, in a voice slightly above a whisper, said, "Giddy up, mule," and out came the stump. Then he turned to the other fellow standing there with his mouth wide open and explained, "You do, but ye gotta get his attention first."

Of course, I've never struck a player, but I *have* raised my voice to the best of them. But on every coaching staff I've been associated with, we've used the old game we learned from our friends in the law-enforcement business—"Good cop—Bad cop." If I had to lose my pleasantness while clarifying a coaching point to some stubborn player, one of the other coaches automatically knew that he had better walk off the field with his arm around that player's shoulder explaining how "Old Coach Meadows" was just trying to make him a better player.

I'll have to say that the coaches' old nemesis, summertime, is much easier to deal with in the realm of modern-day football than it was when I started my journey up and down the sidelines. With the seven-on-seven tournaments, quarterback/receiver camps, and other individualized position camps, coupled with up-to-date weight rooms, the coach has many more tools at his disposal to aid him in keeping those young minds focused on him and that football season that is always just around the corner.

CHAPTER 13

Getting It All Together

Practice Schedule

I don't believe that practice schedules should be set in concrete. There are successful coaches who do everything on a timer and will not vary from it. I never have had a rigid schedule because I've always been someone who believes that when I see something that is "broken," I need to fix it right then. If a mistake is made during a scrimmage or drill, I want the person who made it to be coached while it is fresh on his and the coach's mind. A rigid schedule does not allow for sufficient time to adequately correct all the mistakes that *will* be made in the course of an afternoon's practice. The outcome of close games is usually decided by the *little things*. Through the years, I found that when I had an experienced team, I didn't need to hit that much—just polish and perfect. If I had a new bunch of inexperienced players, I would have one of those controlled scrimmages almost every day after individual drill time. Many days, my practice plan after all the team was on the field was "Down there and back—Huddle up!"

I am a firm believer that your practice schedule must be adjustable from year to year, week to week, and even day to day. I have adjusted mine thirty minutes after we hit the field if things weren't going to suit me. I always had a mental picture of what we needed to accomplish during each practice. My assistants and I spent several hours from Friday night until Monday morning breaking down our film and then the opponent's film. At times, obtaining the opponent's film was more difficult than at other times. I have mentioned the importance of maintaining a good rapport with those other coaches on your schedule since this definitely will facilitate your scouting procedure and game preparation.

I don't recall at what coaching clinic I picked up this following pre-game walk- through, but I believe that it is the most comprehensive I've seen. It covers most every situation that you might encounter in a game. We practiced all of the special situations in the off-season, at the beginning of summer practice, and then every day during drill time. There is nothing more embarrassing than to have one of these circumstances occur and you're not prepared for it. I've always gone out in shorts and shoulder pads on Thursday and with proper organization, I can cover this entire package in thirty-five to forty minutes:

Pre-Game Walk-Through

_____ vs _____
                                                                DATE_____

(1) KICKOFF-RETURN TEAM (Scout Kickoff Team)
    Ball to 35-yard line

(2) OFFENSE (Scout Defense)
    Ball On
    MD 35 1st Down + 2 Play_____
    RH 37 2nd Down + 8 Play_____
    LH 45 1st Down + 1 Play_____
    MD 46 2nd Down + 3 Play_____
    RH 49 3rd Down + 1 Play_____

(3) PUNT TEAM (Scout Defense)
    MD 50 4th Down— PUNT TEAM— PUNT: Spread or Regular

(4) DEFENSE (Scout Offense)
    MD 20 1st Down + 3 Defense_____
    LH 23 2nd Down + 3 Defense_____
    RH 26 3rd Down + 2 Defense_____

(5) PUNT RETURN (Scout Punt)
    MD 28—Punt
    Return: R / L / M   Ball to 50-yard line

(6) OFFENSE (Scout Defense)
    LH 50 1st Down + 5 Play_____
    MD 45 2nd Down + 5 Play_____
    RH 40 1st Down + 5 Play_____
    MD 35 2nd Down + 5 Play_____
    RH 30 1st Down + 30 Play_____ (Score)

(7) EXTRA POINT (Scout Block)

(8) KICKOFF TEAM (Scout Return)

(9) DEFENSE (Scout Offense)
    MD 20 1st Down + 5 Defense_____
    LH 25 2nd Down + 4 Defense_____
    MD 29 3rd Down NG Defense_____

(10) PUNT RETURN* (Scout Punt)
  * <u>Punt Block</u>

(11) OFFENSE (Scout Defense)
  MD   30   1st Down + 5   Play_____
  LH   35   2nd Down + 4   Play_____
  MD   39   3rd Down + 11   Play (Fake Punt)

(12) FAKE PUNT

(13) OFFENSE (Scout Defense)
  MD   50   1st Down + 5   Play_____
  LH   45   2nd Down + 15   Play_____
  MD   30   1st Down + 30   Play_____ (Score)

(14) 2-POINT CONVERSION –<u>Need at least 3</u>—(Scout Defense)

(15) ON-SIDE KICK (Scout Return)

(16) GOAL-LINE DEFENSE (Scout Offense)
  MD   7   1st Down + 2   Defense_____
  LH   5   2nd Down + 2   Defense_____
  MD   3   3rd Down + 1   Defense_____

(17) FIELD-GOAL BLOCK
  MD   2   4th Down—Field-Goal Block Team

(18) COMING-OUT OFFENSE (Scout Defense)
  MD   1   1st Down + 2   Play_____
  LH   3   2nd Down + 2   Play_____
  MD   5   3rd Down   NG   Play_____

(19) TAKE A SAFETY
  RH   5   4th Down   Play_____

(20) KICKOFF / PUNT AFTER SAFETY

(21) DEFENSE (Scout Offense)
  MD   50   1st Down + 2   Defense_____
  RH   45   2nd Down + 5   Defense_____
  MD   43   3rd Down + 2   Defense_____
  MD   41   4th Down   (Long Field-Goal Attempt)

(22) DEFENSE (RETURN FIELD-GOAL ATTEMPT)

(23) COMING-OUT OFFENSE
    RH   1   1st Down + 2   Play_____
    MD   3   2nd Down + 2   Play_____

(24) QUICK KICK
    LH   5   3rd Down   Play <u>QUICK KICK</u>

(25) PUNT-RETURN TEAM (Scout Punt from End Zone)
    Fair Catch—Free Kick for Field Goal

(26) PREVENT DEFENSE (Scout Offense)
    Opponent's Pass Offense

(27) OFFENSE (TWO-MINUTE OFFENSE) TD? / FG RANGE?
    Ball on 25-yard line—3 Timeouts—2:43 left in game
        A. Get all you can get—<u>GET OUT OF BOUNDS</u>
        B. Clock—Clock—Clock—Line up in last formation—QB—Spike ball
        C. Clock stops on 1st Down
        D. QB—Look to sidelines after every play

(28) FIELD GOAL (FAKE FIELD GOAL)

(29) GOOD-HANDS RETURN (Scout Kick)
    Field On-Side Kick

(30) VICTORY FORMATION
    Favorite Play!

Part XI

The Reason That It All Came To Pass

The Number One Key to My Success

I've been asked a hundred times over my career, "To what number one thing do you attribute the success that you've had in coaching?" To answer that question with one brief statement is as difficult as standing at the head table at your football banquet and trying to thank all of those responsible for that gala event. Invariably, you will leave out one or two of your most staunch supporters. Success, in any sports endeavor, is the product of many dedicated people and an enormous amount of skilled preparation that create events and circumstances that have as the ultimate conclusion the desired result. Winning in athletics is very similar to building a fine automobile. It doesn't begin on the showroom floor with the smooth-talking salesman but somewhere in a dirty steel mill with hundreds of people and events in between. As the head coach it will be by *your* name that the victories and the defeats will be recorded, but just as with the fancy car—you're just the salesman.

Having said all of that, I can easily answer the question of what has been the *main* factor that has made me successful—my wife of fifty-six years—Glenda Blake Meadows. When you, as a coach or as a prospective coach, choose a mate, be certain that she realizes that she not only is marrying one man for life but also that she is hosting fifty to a hundred teenage boys a year who will suddenly become a huge part of her existence. Their performance every Friday night from August to December will dictate everything from where you live (and for how long)—to how you're treated in the grocery store—to the day-to-day demeanor of your spouse. In my early years, schools didn't have a film room where we could congregate the entire squad to grade their performance or to break down an opponent play by play. Almost every night of the week, hundreds of feet of 16mm celluloid were run through my old Kodak Analyst in front of scores of muscled-up teenagers and four or five overweight coaches. If my wife had a dollar for every time she heard the expression "Run that back" uttered by a wound-up coach or an excited player, she could match the wealth of Mrs. John D. Rockefeller instead of the meager assets of "Ol' John L. Meadows." Even with the inevitable broken chairs, soiled couches, frayed carpet, and the countless spur-of-the-moment meals and snacks, the only complaint I recall from my "number one assistant" and companion usually had to do with my passing when I should have run or running when I should have passed. Although she gave life to only four children, she was very much involved in the raising of hundreds. In the eyes of the world, the success of a coach is measured by the number of *wins* that he amasses in his career, but the victory that I cherish the most is *winning the heart of Miss Glenda Blake* who—win, lose, or draw—has been by my side as a constant source of support and encouragement.